156 Ways to
Free Your
Creative Spirit

ART AND SOUL

PAM GROUT

**Andrews McMeel
Publishing**
Kansas City

00 01 02 03 04 RDC 10 9 8 7 6 5 4 3 2 1

Library of Congress Cataloging-in-Publication Data

Grout, Pam.
    Art and soul : 156 ways to free your creative spirit / Pam Grout.
        p. cm.
    ISBN 0-7407-0482-6 (hardcover)
    1. Creative ability—Problems, exercises, etc. 2. Creation (Literary, artistic, etc.) I. Title.
    BF408 .G697 2000
    153.3'5—dc21   99-055736
                                                                   CIP
Design and composition by Mauna Eichner
Illustrations on pages 25, 149, 249, and 264 by Tanya Maiboroda

---

ATTENTION: SCHOOLS AND BUSINESSES

Andrews McMeel books are available at quantity discounts with bulk purchase for educational, business, or sales promotional use. For information, please write to: Special Sales Department, Andrews McMeel Publishing, 4520 Main Street, Kansas City, Missouri 64111.

Say yes if you're an artist.
Say yes if you've known it from
the beginning of time.

RUMI

This book is dedicated to my Poetry and Soul group—

Bob Savino

Jesse Bretthorst

Joannes Sikora

Nancy Shurle

Mary Beth Howe-Bernhardt

Carlton K. Logan

Connie Rodriquez

and all the other brilliant poets,
authors, painters, and mandolin players
who have experienced the magic.

Thank You, Thank You

He keeps sending me angels
From up on high
He keeps sending me angels
To teach me to fly
He keeps sending me angels
Just like you.

Jerry Lynn Williams and Frankie Miller wrote those words, Kathy Mattea sang them, and I am choosing to steal them because they say exactly what I feel about the many angels who flew into my life with kind words, moral support, and just the right idea when I needed it most.

The biggest, wet-kissed thank you goes to Kitty Shea, who took this manuscript at a time when it was little but a pile of rough musings and I was a card-carrying basket case. She read every word at least twice, pasted stickers in the margins, sketched hearts with such sentiments as "Me + Art Forever," and gave me so many excellent suggestions that I should probably name her as coauthor. Kitty, you never were unflavored gelatin.

Also, thanks to Wendy Druen, who also volunteered to read early drafts, and to Bob Mendoza, who listened to every word over his car phone while chauffeuring celebrities, business executives, and teenage prom queens around in his limousine. Thanks to Unity Church of Overland Park, Ronnie DeWitt, and my beautiful daughter, Tasman, whose wild spirit continually reminds me of what's best and sweetest in life.

What if imagination and art are not frosting at all,
but the fountainhead of human experience?
ROLLO MAY

Table of Contents

THE ESSAYS

Inspiring stuff to remind
you who you are.

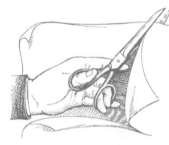

WEEKLY PROJECTS

This is where we cut and paste.

And cut and paste some more.

You're in Good Company

A tiny reminder that you're
no different than Tom Hanks.

Introduction

All my life, I've been a closet bohemian. Even though I grew up in a small Kansas town, was a minister's daughter, a straight-A student, and a goody-two-shoes, I always longed to live big, be outrageous.

Outside, I was Pam Grout, junior achiever. But inside, I have always been Isadora Duncan.

Glimpses of this alter ego snuck out whenever possible. In junior high, I wore Roy Rogers pajamas to a church bake sale, telling customers that our youth group was raising money to send me to a "special home." This was done, I might add, without the approval of my minister father.

I roller-skated through my high school wearing a clown suit and a mask of Richard Nixon. In college, I again donned a mask and roller skates, only this time I wore a bikini and a signboard that read, "Follow me to Hoove's-A-Go-Go."

After college, I tried the corporate world but quickly discovered that bosses tend to frown on thongs and high-top tennis shoes. I took to writing travel articles and personality profiles about people who make houses out of rolled-up newspapers, people who collect nuts and make films about guinea pigs.

As much as I like St. Francis of Assisi, I have come to the conclusion that I like wild people better. People who hug trees, ride Harleys, pierce their noses. People who live outside the bell curve. Either side of the bell curve.

Despite these glaring aberrations, I still feel like unflavored gelatin much of the time. Yes, I want to suck the marrow out of life, be Zorba the Greek. But at the same time, I want people to like me.

So I follow the rules. Mow my lawn. Watch my feet to make sure I'm doing it right.

I woke up one day to discover that my bold Isadora Duncan self had given way to a rote, lonely life. Instead of running with the wolves, I found I was crawling with the lemmings. My zany ideas, my outrageous dreams had been left to languish in the crisp green lawns of suburbia.

I don't really know how it happened. I don't know who this "they say" really is. It's like the frog and the water. You can't toss him in when the water's boiling. He'd jump out faster than you could say "french-fried frog legs." But if you turn the heat up slowly, degree by tiny degree, he doesn't even notice he's being boiled alive.

Likewise, if "they"—whoever "they" are—tried to boil our originality out of us in one fell swoop, we'd put up our dukes immediately. But degree by tiny degree, we agree to conform, abandoning everything that's fun and original and authentically "us."

This book is about breaking free, about jumping out of the boiling water no matter how long you've been cooking.

I've heard that we teach what we want to know. In this case, I'm teaching what I want to do. I want to dress in angel costumes, travel without a suitcase, get up in the morning and decide who I am and what I want to be. I want to hang with other bohemians, people who value big ideas over big homes.

2

I want to meet friends in cafés to write. I want to spend Saturday nights painting on walls, hosting show-and-tells, and playing charades. I want to share my dancing, daring, audacious side.

For years, I denied this side. I focused on this other person, this impostor who wasn't really me. In fact, I was so busy doing affirmations, reading books, and trying to heal this broken-down impostor that I sorta forgot that the real me, the crazy, quirky, lightning-bug me was the very thing I'd been searching for.

I hope *Art and Soul* is the very thing you've been searching for. It's about making art, yes. But it's also about becoming more, about recapturing that authentic self that many of us abandoned along with the Crayola crayons. Maybe yours isn't as bohemian or as far out as mine (after all, creativity comes in all sorts of packages), but all of us have an authentic self that, over the years, has been broken into thousands of pieces just like our once-favorite blue-green crayon.

In a nutshell, *Art and Soul* is an apprenticeship, an actual year-long journey into your creative soul. You may have already decided that you're a writer or a painter or a dancer, but I say, "Don't choose. Don't limit. Just do."

Each of the fifty-two weeks has an inspirational message, a creative project, and three or four more suggested "fun stuff."

Yes, it's Richard Simmons for the brain, but more important, *Art and Soul* is the call to a spiritual path. Not only do we ask God to help us become more alive, but we trust that creating is our spiritual destiny, the road that leads us to enlightenment.

Unlike some books that encourage you to uncover all the negative gunk that stops you from creating, this book moves right to the heart: Just do it! Not only are there all kinds of offbeat, original activities like chalking poems on sidewalks and staging poetry readings around campfires, but each week you'll create one major project like a short story, a self-portrait, or a song.

There isn't a lot of instruction; this is by design. One of the main threads running through this book is "you already know how."

3

You've been to enough workshops. You've read enough books. Doing art is in your bones. It's in your makeup. You simply need to show up, listen, and take action. God will take care of the rest.

Author Bernie Siegel once went through a guided meditation to make contact with his "inner guide." Since he was a medical doctor and a prominent author, he figured he'd get somebody famous, somebody like Moses or Abraham. Instead, he got some guide named Frank.

Well, this time you get a guide named Pam, but I reckon between the two of us, God, and our prancing, creative spirits, we can do most anything.

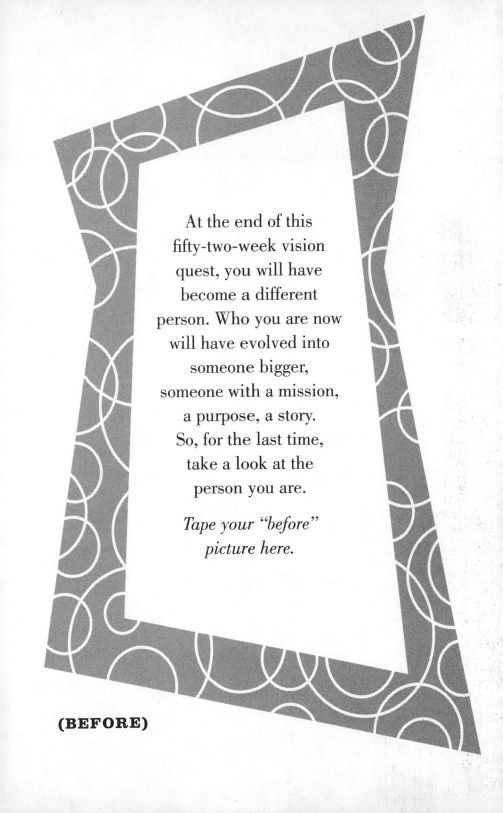

At the end of this
fifty-two-week vision
quest, you will have
become a different
person. Who you are now
will have evolved into
someone bigger,
someone with a mission,
a purpose, a story.
So, for the last time,
take a look at the
person you are.

*Tape your "before"
picture here.*

(BEFORE)

This little light of mine, I'm going to let it shine.

CHRISTIAN SPIRITUAL

SHINING LIGHT

Most books tell you how to get something—a sizzling sex life, thinner thighs, a higher return on your investment dollar. *Art and Soul* is a book that tells you how to give, how to reach deep inside yourself and pull out the artistic blessing that is yours to give. The blessing that no one else can give.

Maybe it's a poem tapping on your heart. Maybe there's a song that keeps you awake at night, a screenplay that won't leave you alone. A dream you keep pushing aside with some comment like "Nah! I could never sing or dance like that. I could never make a film."

Now is the time to quit pushing that dream aside.

Every dream that has ever tiptoed across your mind is a summons from God—a summons that says, "I need you."

On the day you were born, God presented you with a creative gift. It is a gift the world needs. Maybe your song won't be sung on David Letterman. It may never make the Top Forty list. But somebody out there needs to hear it. Maybe it's the ninety-two-year-old shut-in who lives next door, who giggles every time she overhears you sing, "I Wish I Were an Oscar Mayer Wiener" outside her bedroom window. Isn't that enough?

At times, it seems like a daunting task, adding your voice to the chorus. You wonder:

"What do I have to add to the world's great body of art?"

"Who am I to join the likes of Bette Midler, Mikhail Baryshnikov, Peter Ustinov?"

Perhaps the better question is:

"Who are you *not* to? What right do you have to refuse the voice that whispers to you every morning, every afternoon, and every evening as you retire spent and exhausted from denying again and again the hand of the Great Collaborator?"

"But hasn't everything already been said?"

Until we hear your version of this fierce and joyful world, there is more to be said. Each man looks upon the sunset with a slightly different eye.

All of us long for a rich, participatory life. We all have the same recurrent longing to break down our defenses, to be able to give and receive our gifts. When we compose a piece of music or shape a lump of clay, we wriggle out of the straitjacket and come out shouting, "Yes, yes, yes!" to the possibilities of Spirit.

Alexander Papaderos, who started a monastery and Peace Center in Crete, Greece, carries a piece of a broken mirror in his wallet. When he was a small boy, he found the broken mirror next to a motorcycle that someone had wrecked and then abandoned along a road near his small village. He spent hours trying to put the mirror back together. Unfortunately, some of the pieces were missing so he had little choice but to give up, but not before plucking out the biggest piece, which he rubbed against a rock until it was smooth and round. Papaderos spent much of his childhood playing with that piece of mirror. He discovered that when he held it just right, he could shine the sun's light into the dark, lighting up unknown cracks and crevices.

That's what this book is all about. Your piece of the mirror is just a fragment. Nobody knows for sure how big and vast *the whole* really is. But if you take your small piece and hold it just right, you can shine light into the world's dark places.

The choice is yours. You can use your mirror to shine light. Or you can keep it in your wallet. But the mirror will never be whole without you.

MAKE AN ART AND SOUL BADGE

Declare It and Wear It

You'll probably recognize your fellow artists by the gleam in their eye. They look bouncier somehow, more joyful and playful. They don't quite fit the mold that the rest of society has tried to squish them into.

But just so the rest of the world will know, make yourself an amulet—a special pin or tie or something—that identifies yourself as an *Art and Soul* participant. Proclaim to the world that you are an artist.

More Fun Stuff

Go to a thrift store and buy the most outrageous outfit you can.

Learn three little-known facts about Martin Luther King, Jr.

Make sugar cookies shaped like body parts.

You're in Good Company

(In this section each week, you'll find a short anecdote about a well-known artist, an artist who is successful, who has "made it." I call this part of the book "You're in Good Company" because you'll quickly come to realize that "real artists" are just like you—just as human, just as scared.)

Even with all his success, Steven Spielberg still suffers from insecurity. He says it's like having big ears—it doesn't change just because you win an Oscar.

What can be gained by sailing to the moon if we are not able to cross the abyss that separates us from ourselves? This is the most important of all voyages of discovery and without it all the rest are not only useless but disastrous. **THOMAS MERTON**

CREATE OR DIE

In the next sixty minutes, forty people in this country will try to kill themselves. Four of them will be successful. By the time you finish reading this chapter, one of your brothers will be dead—not from cancer, not from a worn-out heart, but from the unbearable burden of his own pain, the weight of which finally convinced him to place a gun to his precious temple or a razor blade to the wrist that his own mother held as she taught him to walk.

Something, in case you didn't notice, is very wrong with this picture. The fact that one out of every seven women in this country takes Prozac should be a hint to all of us that something has careened completely out of control.

Something sacred has been violated. The human soul has lost faith.

Slowly, over time, we have given up our inheritance. We have turned over our power to think for ourselves, to make things up, to imagine, to plan, and to dream. What do we do instead? Call Pizza Hut and grab the remote control.

God gave us his most precious gift—the ability to create. He gave us the power to conceive the most beautiful worlds, to ordain our own destiny.

Inside each and every one of us is a master chef, an inventor, a writer, a statesman. All these heroes, these immense giants that exist within our souls, are literally dying from boredom. They're sick to death of watching *Days of Our Lives*.

The age of convenience food, cable TV, and ready-made everything is holding hostage the gods within us. It's no wonder we're all depressed. We, the greatest of all creators, with capabilities to build cities and inspire nations, are squandering our time watching reruns of *I Love Lucy*.

We have forgotten that whole galaxies exist within our grasp. We are gods playing fools. Our deepest impulse is to create. Without it, life becomes sterile, little but rote recitation.

I'm not fool enough to suggest that something as simple as writing a poem or singing a song will change the suicide rate in this country. I'm not proposing that we trade in our Prozac for sketchbooks.

But it's a start.

The very act of creating is an act of power, an act of hope. It's a reminder that we are not powerless pawns, not cattle in a big cosmic slaughterhouse. Writing a song or drawing the vase with the wilted delphiniums is a reminder that we *can* do something, a reminder that we have the power to make something from nothing. And as those reminders add up, as hope begins to grow, we no longer feel overwhelmed by our troubles, by the troubles of the world. We remember that we, as humans, as cocreators with God, have immense power to change things.

It is our responsibility to bear witness to the pulse and beauty of life. Our only job is to discover and sing our own song.

You can answer the summons. Or you can die.

13

COME UP WITH THE TITLE OF YOUR AUTOBIOGRAPHY

The World According to Pam

Rick Bragg called his *All Over But the Shoutin'*. Roy Blount, Jr., called his hilarious memoir of growing up *Be Sweet: A Conditional Love Story*. Katharine Hepburn, who happens to be famous enough to get away with it, called hers simply *Me*. Tina Turner's is *I, Tina*. What are you going to call yours?

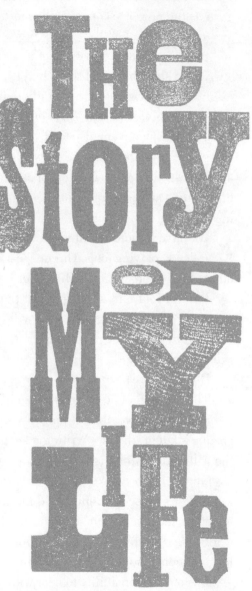

More Fun Stuff

Invent a new type of soup.

Name a rock band.

Paint your fingernails ten different colors.

You're in Good Company

Donald Sutherland has made more than one hundred films, but he still gets so nervous he throws up every time before filming begins.

WEEK 3

The real power behind whatever success
I have now was something I found within
myself—something that's in all of us,
I think, a little piece of God just waiting
to be discovered. **TINA TURNER**

"IT'S EVERYWHERE, IT'S EVERYWHERE"

If you're like most people, you think of creativity as a private
club, reserved like that corner table by the window for a talented
few. You believe it's passed out at birth to the Bachs, the Matisses,
the James Camerons of the world.

You, on the other hand (*sigh!*), are fated to be a consumer of
creativity, decorating your foyer with *other* people's sculptures,
spending your evenings watching *other* people's visions on a
twenty-six-inch screen.

But the truth is all of us are creative. All of us have the ability
to create new ideas, solve baffling problems, even produce art.

It's why we sing in the shower, why we write jokes in the dirt
on unwashed cars.

In case you didn't hear, you were created in the image and the
likeness of the Big Creative Kahuna. Whatever your thoughts

about God (and I know, lots of us think of Him as this judgmental old toad who sits up in heaven just salivating for the chance to mark down "naughty, naughty" in His big, black book), you can't really deny that a good percentage of the world believes He'd probably include "creative" on his list of credentials.

Who else would bother to make every snowflake different? Every fingerprint on all ten fingers of the world's six billion people unique? Even bugs, the lowliest of the species, have been given great creative consideration. In the beetle family alone, there are more than 300,000 varieties.

Just like the barber who passes his scissors and razors down to his son, God has passed this "ability to create" down to us. Just like the engineer who smiles when his son builds a bridge out of his blocks, God smiles when we write poems.

Most of us can accept that being like God means being kind, being compassionate, giving canned creamed corn to people less fortunate. But God, more than anything else, wants us to create, to express, to be more like Him. It is not only our right to create, but our responsibility and eventual destiny.

When you buy a computer, it's bundled with all sorts of software programs—a word-processing program, a program to access the Internet, a program for figuring your finances. Human beings, like computers, are also bundled with certain software packages. We all come with the "program" to produce children, to think, and to fall in love. Another program that's installed in every one of us is the creativity package.

At this point, it may be like PowerPoint or Excel on my computer, dormant and unused. But just like the icon that's there in the right-hand corner of my computer screen awaiting the day I take my mouse and point it to the appropriate place, your creativity package is there awaiting your say-so.

The other day, Tasman, my five-year-old, said, "Mom, do all tadpoles grow into frogs?"

I was stumped for a minute. Some of them probably don't—

17

they get squished by a lawn mower, can't find enough flies, or run up against some other tadpole deterrent. But this I could tell her without hesitation: Every single tadpole is encoded with the ability to "be a frog."

Might as well start croaking.

WRITE AND TELL A JOKE

Did You Hear the One About . . . ?

Woody Allen wanted to be a magician until he discovered he could write one-liners for the New York tabloids. While still in high school, he was hired to write jokes. For three hours each day after school, he could easily come up with three or four typewritten pages with fifty-some jokes.

So you never know where a good joke could lead you. My friend Todd started writing jokes—things like "she had more chins than the Chinese phone book"—and ended up touring the country as a stand-up comic.

Use newspaper headlines for inspiration. Look how many jokes Monica Lewinsky inspired!

More people view credit as the lay-awake plan.

You know you've hit middle age when you wake up feeling bad and you did absolutely nothing the night before.

Invite someone from a foreign country
to tea.

Look through the want ads and find a job
that you clearly aren't qualified for but
might like if you were. Compose a cover
letter telling your future employer why
you'd like the job. Stick it in the mail with
your résumé.

Make a puzzle.

You're in Good Company

Thirteen publishers turned down William Kennedy's
Pulitzer prize–winning novel, *Ironweed*.

Creativity Test

There's the SAT to see if you're bright enough to get into college, the LSAT to see if you can make it in law school, the MCAT, which opens doors to med school.

But here, being offered for absolutely no charge, is the very best test I know for measuring creativity in human beings.

Get out your pencil.

Pam Grout's
Test of Creativity

1. Are you breathing?

Yes _____   No _____

Check your score here.

If you answered "yes" to the above question, you're highly creative.

WEEK 4

The concept of creativeness and the concept of the healthy,
self-actualizing, fully human person seem to be coming closer and closer
together, and may perhaps turn out to be the same thing.

ABRAHAM MASLOW

YOU SAY YOU WANT A REVOLUTION . . .

If you're under thirty-five, you may not remember the physical fitness revolution. Or rather you may not remember life before the
pump-it, dance-it, just-do-it days. Back then, it was not only ac-
ceptable to be a couch potato, it was really the only option.

The only people who really "worked out" were professional
athletes. The rest of us never considered the idea that we too
needed physical exercise.

But then Dr. Kenneth Cooper coined the term *aerobics* and
proposed the radical notion that everyone should exercise. Today,
of course, there's not an American alive who doesn't either engage
in some sort of physical activity or at least feel guilty because he
doesn't.

This same kind of revolution is happening with our brains—
our creative muscle, if you will. We're finally figuring out that it's
not just professional artists who need creativity. If we are to survive as a species, all of us must exercise our creativity. Just as our
bodies atrophy when we don't use them, so do our creative minds.

Creativity is imperative to a full, growing life. You're missing something big if you're not growing your mind.

When we don't practice being creative, our brains go limp and lifeless. We become prone to repeating ourselves. And repeating ourselves. And repeating . . .

It's estimated that we have 60,000 thoughts each day. A pretty impressive statistic until you hear this one—95 percent of those thoughts are the same ones we had yesterday. We will never solve our world problems this way. We simply must pry ourselves from our limited, habitual thinking.

The mind, scientists tell us, is virtually unlimited. Your body, on the other hand, can do only so much. Yeah, an 80-pound weakling can turn himself into an Arnold Schwarzenegger or a former couch potato can become athlete of the year, but without a little boost from steroids, genetics, and damned fool hard-headedness, a body has glaring limitations.

A mind, on the other hand, can take you anywhere. It can write a story that can change someone's life. It can inspire a nation, design a building, compose a song.

What's more, this growing, thriving mind-set is the brain's natural state. It was designed to think and create and grow. A liver processes toxins, a heart pumps blood, and a brain thinks big, bounteous thoughts.

It is my dream that *Art and Soul* will launch a revolution as big as the physical fitness revolution of the '60s. I envision secretaries meeting over lunch hours to share poems, and friends making dates to write together in cafés, Saturday night paintfests where paper is taped to the wall, aprons are passed out, and people paint, not talk.

Already, there are pockets of people doing creative, satisfying, celebratory things.

In Paonia, Colorado, for example, there's a little storefront in the middle of downtown called the Sage Stage. Every Friday night, the residents of this fruit-growing community on the western slope of Colorado get together to perform for one another. One guy might play his guitar. The next recites a poem. Those who don't play or read show up to cheer and to hatch plans for next week, when they'll be up there, strutting their stuff.

We all need to strut our stuff. That is why we were created.

In Seattle, Washington, there's a troupe of artists called God Only Knows What. Using skits, music, comedy, dance, and improvisation, these six artists write and perform three or four shows a year.

So what if they're not in *People* magazine. Success, as far as I'm concerned, should be measured by pleasure, wholeness, and a sense of self-esteem.

Art is a tool for living, a spiritual calling. It doesn't matter who you are, how old you are, or where you come from. A creative life will lead you out into the country, where it is wild, tangled, and rich.

A hundred years ago, we didn't need to jog or swim laps because most of us worked on a farm, digging turnips and planting corn. We got enough aerobic exercise in day-to-day living. Likewise, our ancestors exercised their creativity in their day-to-day lives. When they finished plowing the garden, they pulled out the family banjo and sang songs or they gathered around the hearth to tell stories. There was no such thing as thirty-two-screen movie cinemas and radios to play the Top Forty.

This week, we're going to take back the reins of creativity. We don't need some publisher to tell us we're worthy of publication, some record producer to decide whether or not our songs are "up to contemporary American standards." Creativity belongs to all of us. Do I hear an "Amen!"?

ACT OUT A SCENE FROM
THE WIZARD OF OZ

Lions and Tigers and Bears, Oh My!

Yes, you're going to need friends. Somebody's got to be the Tin Man, the Scarecrow, and the Cowardly Lion. Maybe you'll even want a Toto or a Wicked Witch. You pick the scene. You pick the cast. Remember, however, that this week you're an actor, a singer, and maybe even a wizard.

Make five styles of paper airplanes.
See which one flies best.

Make your own coloring book.

Try a Buddhist meditation ritual.

You're in Good Company

The Beatles were turned down by producers at Decca Records because "guitar groups were on their way out."

YOU ALREADY KNOW HOW

The first thing most of us do when we want to pursue a new art is find a class, buy a book, seek out the advice of an "expert." While there's certainly a time and place for outside help, that's not the first place to turn.

When we go outside seeking direction, we create at least two hurdles. The obvious one is the time we waste. Instead of leaping in when the idea is fresh, when its voice demands to be heard, we put it off, insist that it be patient and wait until we learn how to punctuate our sentences or mix our paint. We ask this burning, passionate idea that wants nothing but to dance and scream to sit quietly outside the door and wait.

But it can't wait. It needs to be heard now. It's crying out today. How can you put an exploding volcano on hold? How can you tell a raging river to wait patiently while you learn what a preposition is?

Think of the idea that's knocking on your door as a small child. It can't understand that grown-ups have other things to do.

"But," you insist, "I really *don't* know how. I have never written an article, let alone a book. I have never created a character, let alone a whole play. I've got to get help."

This may sound like a rational plea. But I assure you, it's only a stall tactic. Sure, your reason for waiting may seem reasonable and mature, but you're dealing with an idea that is anything but reasonable and mature. In fact, if you do wait, it will become reasonable and mature, but by then it's too late. Who wants to see a reasonable and mature sculpture? A reasonable and mature stage play?

The juice, the gas, has turned into an adult.

You can polish your skills later—after the idea that's pounding in your skull is aired. Get it down now.

Waiting until you "know how" can take a week if you read a book, a semester if you take a class, a lifetime if you perfect a skill. By then, the idea is stiff, lifeless, nothing but a scab. It has faded like the old gingham curtains hanging in the kitchen window.

Once the fire is gone, we have a great excuse not to write it at all or if we do persist, we get discouraged by the stiffness and wonder where we missed the boat. Guess we should take another class.

It's imperative that we answer the questions when they're first asked. Otherwise, the question has no choice but to look elsewhere. It must find someone who has the time and the confidence to carry the torch.

Go ahead. Jump in. Get your feet wet. Place your faith in the idea itself. Trust in the story, the dance, the painting. They have the ability to teach you anything you need to know. Within their fiery beat are the questions *and* the answers. If you surrender to them, they will take you home.

Sam Shepard, who has written more than forty plays and even

won a Pulitzer Prize in 1979 for his play *Buried Child*, was twenty-one when he wrote his first two plays, *Cowboys* and *Rock Garden*. As a young artist living in New York, he had no formal theater training and no exposure to dramatic literature. Luckily for him, he was too young and inexperienced to question whether or not he knew how to write a play. Nobody had told him yet that people don't write a new play every two weeks. So he did. He listened to the fierce male characters playing hopscotch in his head. If he'd have said, "Hey, guys, I hear you, but I'm kinda busy right now with this class I need to take. I'll go to the library tomorrow and see if I can find a book," the American theater scene would be missing forty controversial and poignant plays. He let the characters and the plays speak. He let them teach him how.

Passion, love, that burning fire—these will create your art, not the skills you learn in a book.

Pablo Neruda, the Spanish poet, always said that poetry found him. He didn't read a how-to book. He didn't go to college to study meter and rhyme. The poetry, he says, arrived. His only job was to walk through the portal, shake hands, and invite it in.

The art form that's calling to you has all the answers you will ever need. It wants to be your partner.

Don't head off to the bookstore. Don't call the college to see when the next gouache class is. Start now.

COMPOSE A POEM

Roses are red

It might help to put on a red beret. Or grow one of those shaggy beards. Get into the spirit of it. It can be a rhyming poem, a haiku, or a poem that expresses your frustrations. Just make sure you write something.

On the next page, you'll find a poem I wrote, a takeoff on the popular Dr. Seuss book *Green Eggs and Ham*. If nothing else, it should take away all your frustrations about not being "good enough" or "not knowing how to do it." I had never written a poem when I wrote this one for one of my creativity classes.

Green Eggs and Pam

I am Pam.
Pam, I am.

I did not like that Pam, I am.
Who always said, "yes sir," "yes, ma'am."
And kept her real self on the lam.

I did not like that Pam, I am.
I did not like "yes, sir," "yes, ma'am."

I longed to step out of my box.
To dance, to scream, to be a fox.

I did not like "yes sir," "yes, ma'am."
I did not like them.
Pam, I am.

But would I? Could I?
Break the bars?
Would I? Could I? Reach the stars?

Not in my box.
Not as a fox.
Not while I'm trembling
In fear of the gawks.

I might like her.
I will see.
I might like just being me.

But would I? Could I?
Break through the fear?
Be now. Be here.
Date Richard Gere.

Try it. Try it.
And I may see.
I might just like it, being me.

Say!
I like that Pam, I am.
I do. I like her.
Pam, I am.

I even like her when in pain.
And in the dark.
And in the rain.

And as a star. And up a tree.
She is so me, so me, you see.

I do so like that Pam, I am.
Thank you. Thank you.
Pam, I am.

More Fun Stuff

Catch a jar of fireflies.
(If it's winter, make a snow angel.)

Wear nothing but yellow or purple or blue.

See how many Christmas carols you can remember.

You're in Good Company

Rodin failed three times to secure admittance to the school of art he wished to attend. His uncle called him uneducable and his father said, "I have an idiot for a son."

Aren't you tired of only doing things you already know how to do?

Week 6

But there it sits, nevertheless, calmly licking its chops.

H. L. MENCKEN

NIKE WAS RIGHT

Once you get a feel for this book, you'll probably conclude that the important part is the weekly essays. You'll read them with religious fervor, feel inspired, be ready to take on the world. You'll feel sure that you're destined to become a great artist, to produce things that make others drop to their knees.

The weekly projects? Hey, they sound fun too, but I'll do them later—when I have a free moment. Probably tomorrow.

Let me clear something up for you. The weekly essays are not the important part of this book.

Remember the first day of class in the movie *Dead Poets Society*, when Mr. Keating, the English teacher played by Robin Williams, asks his students to open their books to the section on analyzing poetry? After instructing one of the boys to begin reading, Keating jumps wildly out of his chair before the boy even gets to the second sentence. "Rip that introduction out!" he yells to the incredulous students. "It means nothing. That's right. It's horseshit. Be gone with it."

That's how I feel about the essays. I like them. In fact, they were *my* weekly projects for a year. But you'll miss the whole point of this book if you pass on the projects. It'd be like going to the rodeo and ignoring the horses.

Yet I know a lot of you won't do the exercises. Oh, you'll want to. You'll mean to. You'll keep adding it to your "to do" list. But then it gets late. And you're tired. And your very favorite comedian of all time is going to be on Jay Leno . . . and well, you'll just do it . . . tomorrow.

Why do I know this? Because I'm just like you. Ever since I discovered Wayne W. Dyer's *Your Erroneous Zones* in high school, I've been a hopelessly addicted self-help junkie. If I had become all the things I read about becoming, I'd have a Pulitzer Prize, an Oscar, and a note from God saying I was the most functional (as opposed to dysfunctional) person on this planet.

I used to be embarrassed at how many self-help books I'd read. I hid them beneath in-flight magazines when I was flying because I didn't want my seatmate to know I was trying to have a better relationship or to think my way to winning thighs.

Naturally, I refused to display them on my bookshelf. What if somebody saw them? A bookshelf, I've always felt, says something about its owner—like a pair of shoes or the car you drive.

I finally came out of the closet when a therapist pointed out that this "library in my head" was one of my special talents. Who else knows how to do affirmations eighty-nine ways, how to visualize what I want in thirteen languages?

So what I'm trying to say is, I've got your number. That said, let me just reiterate that the exercises are what make this book special. They're the gift, the meat and potatoes.

Now that I'm finally out of the closet, I can tell you that one of the most influential books in my library (and I do display this one proudly on my bookshelf) is the *The Artist's Way* by Julia Cameron.

Twice since the book has come out, I've been in Artist's Way groups. This is a suggestion she made that I actually *did* follow.

She recommends we artists band together and support one another in our various pursuits.

The first time I took the class, a twelve-week course that followed each of the twelve chapters, I loved it. I'd have rather slit my veins in a warm bath than miss the Saturday morning session. I lived for the next week so I could talk about my angst over not writing or how I was shamed as a kid. It was group therapy for artists. Although I loved the group, I don't remember that my output increased. I didn't grow as an artist or become a better writer.

The second time, however, was a different story. First of all, I was facilitating the group. So I had this pressure to actually *be* an artist. Out of frustration on the first day of class (there were so many attendees I couldn't keep track), I asked everyone to make a name tag.

No big deal, right?

Well, ask an artist to make anything and watch out. The results were astounding. Each member brought in a beautiful name tag that expressed his or her uniqueness. In that second class, we spent less time talking about our childhood issues and more time talking about how we decided to make our name tags.

From that point on, we did a project every week. Yeah, we still spent the first hour of our two-hour session talking about our blocks and struggles, but the last hour was spent performing a character or reading a poem or showing a self-portrait.

It was powerful. People started changing. They started actually *doing* their art. It was particularly freeing to work in other media. I, for example, have always billed myself as a writer. So naturally everything I write is supposed to be glorious, grammatically correct, and worthy of great praise. But I could paint and not give a rat's ass what anybody thought.

Once we committed to being there for our art, our muses showed up in full force. They must have been talking among themselves, saying something like, "You know, I think we can count on these people."

37

Brilliant things began to pour forth.

One night, at 3 A.M., a children's book—something I'd never aspired to write—yanked me by the arm. Daniel began painting bright, kicky portraits and got dozens of new commissions. Bonnie started writing poetry that helped her through a nasty divorce. Beth started drawing again after a several-year hiatus.

So that's why it's important you do the activities.

It's fine to dream about painting or writing a stage play, but unless you actually sit down and work at it, nothing is going to change. As Wayne Gretzky says, "You miss 100 percent of the shots you don't take."

INVENT A NEW HOLIDAY.

Merry Pie Day!

My friends Jack and Virginia have custody of their grandson, Roland. One year, while celebrating Father's Day, Roland, who weeks earlier had celebrated Mother's Day, demanded to know when "Kid's Day" was. Not only did it get a big giggle from his grandparents, but it started a brand-new custom in their family. Every year, in the third week of June, the Mocks celebrate Kid's Day. Roland and his sister, Amber, get gifts and a special dinner.

    This week, you too will invent a new holiday.

    Maybe you want a holiday where everyone honors pie by eating pie for breakfast, lunch, and dinner. Maybe you'd like to celebrate Shakespeare's birthday. Come up with some ammunition for your new holiday (maybe you need to do some research at the library) and write a letter to Hallmark Cards (you don't have to send it, unless, of course, you want to) and explain the significance of this new holiday.

    Hallmark's address is 2501 McGee, Kansas City, MO 64108.

Psst! This is it, the important part.

More Fun Stuff

Create a new bar drink.

Paint a pair of old tennis shoes.

Eat breakfast somewhere you've never eaten before.

You're in Good Company

Robin Williams was voted "least likely to succeed" in his high school class.

WEEK seven

Even God can't steer a parked car.

MARY OMWAKE

THE BITTER TRUTH

As much as you want to sit down, grab your paintbrush, and start producing beautiful pieces of art, let me just say that it's probably not going to happen. At first.

When you first commit to this course of daily spirituality, a lot of embarrassing and uncomfortable things are going to happen. It's nothing to be alarmed about. It's just that, right now, you're rusty. You're not used to working on your art.

You have no idea what to paint or write or draw. You probably don't hear a single note from your muse. You just have this faint inkling that you want to create something, this tiny whisper that says you might have something to say.

Let me assure you that you do. You have something important to say, something that the world needs to hear.

That conviction is sometimes enough to keep people going.

Usually it's not.

The cold truth is that there are a lot of alligators in the pond.

This week, we're going to look those enemies straight in the whites of their eyes. We're going to examine what we're up against. What every artist is up against. Even Maya Angelou, the prolific author who has written dozens of books, claims that every time she starts a new one, she experiences the same fear, the same questioning. Can she do it again? It's always a scary proposition.

So picture me as the football coach with a diagram of the opponents in next week's game. Yeah, they're big. Yeah, they're tough. But remember, the Spirit that's whispering is always stronger.

Enemy No. 1—Procrastination. When you first commit to working on your art, you will hear a tiny voice. Or at least you'll think you did. Or you did until the appointed hour arrives. And then it's "What was I thinking? I want to be an artist, but not today. Probably tomorrow." And then you go on living the same life you've been living before, the same life you want to escape from.

When you first begin to hear the artists' call, every single excuse you've ever heard or used will come up. You'd rather do almost anything than work on your art. Collecting discarded toenail clippings will sound like the very highest form of entertainment. You'd rather scrub the kitchen floors or cut the balls off your old woolen sweater than sit down at the computer like you promised yourself.

That's your rut—the life that's not working, the life you want to change. Remember the old adage that as long as you keep doing things the way you used to do them your life is going to be the way it used to be.

Enemy No. 2—Resistance. Change is uncomfortable at first. Especially something this risky. An artist is up on the tightrope. He's willing to say, "Hey, look at me!" He's no longer cowering. No longer hiding. As an artist, you might even go on to be happy and fulfilled and walking the path to your destiny.

Every cell in your body is going to resist. You've suddenly made a 360-degree turn and, just like those muscles that start to hurt when you first start running or aerobicizing, the muscles in your psyche, the ones that are so invested in you doing just what you've already done, are going to put up their dukes. You can count on it.

Expect the conflict, the interruptions, the excuses, the self-doubt.

Anne Lamott says when she sits down to write, she immediately begins to wonder if she needs orthodontia or if the moles on her neck are starting to grow. Once she called her brother to see if he had noticed a new mole on her neck.

Quite wisely, he said, "Annie, get back to work."

Because that's the only thing that will get you through it. There's no other way. You can't will your art to appear. You've got to be there and you've got do it every day.

Think about it. Would you hire an employee that sometimes showed up for work, sometimes didn't? The muses, the creative ethers have lots of stories and songs and paintings to give the world, but they will only work with and through someone who is going to show up for work.

Enemy No. 3—Self-doubt. You'll hate everything you produce. You'll look at whatever it is and think, "This is total shit. I'd better stop. I'd better hide it before anyone, God forbid, should see it."

While you're proving yourself, you're going to get a lot of junk that will embarrass you, that will make you think, "I have no talent."

The good news is it will get better. It will get easier.

Right now, you're like a car stuck in the mud. The car runs just fine, might even be a Rolls-Royce once you wash the mud off to look, but it's going to take a while to get it out of that muddy rut. Or think of coming home from vacation and turning on the water faucet. The brown, slimy liquid isn't what you're after, but it's gotta come out first before the sweet, clear water pours forth.

It takes practice. It takes a lot of time being crippled and scared and not sure why you ever wanted to get involved in this crazy creativity business in the first place.

So just say "Hallelujah!" The more junk you write or draw or paint, the sooner you'll tap into the good stuff.

It's not always pretty. It's not always fun. But there's an angel in that piece of marble. And it's up to you to keep chipping and chiseling and pounding.

WRITE A CHRISTMAS LETTER IN JULY AND SEND IT TO ALL YOUR FRIENDS

We Need a Little Christmas Now . . .

In December when you've got dozens of holiday parties and hundreds of gifts to buy, the last thing you really want to do is write a meaningful Christmas letter. Now that it's July or March or maybe even August, you've got the time to kick off your shoes and really tell the people you love what you're up to, what you think. Maybe you'll even want to decorate it and include photos.

If you think this isn't art, get this: Isabel Allende produced all her novels by pretending she was writing a letter to her mother.

More Fun Stuff

Make a hat out of newspaper.

Write five hundred words about
someone you hate.

Plan a vacation to your favorite
Caribbean island. Make rum punches
and get straw hats to celebrate. Learn
a song from there.

You're in Good Company

Anthony Burgess, author of *A Clockwork Orange*
and dozens of other books, constantly thought about
giving up writing because of the debilitating fear
that his work wasn't good enough. He thought every
book was a failure from the moment the first sentence was written.

WEEK EIGHT

It's not easy being green.

KERMIT THE FROG

The more failures, the more successes. Period.

TOM PETERS

DARE TO BE MEDIOCRE

Okay, now for the good news. You have permission to write, draw, and paint the worst crap in America. Not only do you have blanket amnesty, you have the responsibility to write lots of garbage, paint lots of blobs, and dance like a tin soldier.

When we allow ourselves to be beginners, to be "mediocre," we're opening up the part of us that plunges into new territory. The muse requires nothing less. We have to plug our nose and dive in.

To be a beginner, an artist who "isn't perfect," takes bravery. To make a mess takes balls. Only those who are willing to jump in naked, splash around in the muck and the mire will ever be able to court the muse.

The muse is not about to hook up with some anal-retentive perfectionist who has to be Georgia O'Keeffe or William Shakespeare the first time out. People like that won't take risks. They're

47

cramped and stiff. The muse needs people who are willing to step off the cliff, people who, in short, are willing to look stupid.

Those who want to do it "perfectly" have an agenda, some idea of what perfect is. And the truth is we don't have enough information to judge. We don't *really* know what's good or bad, let alone what's perfect.

Phil Collins says that when Genesis got together, they just started playing. They didn't care if they hit wrong notes or sang off tune. From that freedom came beautiful things.

"If we'd have worried too much what the others thought nothing would have come out," Collins said.

Fun Fact

Antonio Stradivari made some of his best violins from discarded, broken, water-logged oars he found on Venice docks.

When I wrote my fourth book, a self-published weight-loss book that was eventually bought by a big publishing house, I needed a drawing to demonstrate the importance of deep breathing. I drew this primitive woman who bore a striking resemblance to George Washington. To my powers of judging, it was absolutely the worst drawing a person could ever come up with. If I wasn't on a shoestring budget, if I'd had even twenty-five more dollars, I'd have begged some graphic design student to redo it.

Able to console myself with the fact that I was a "writer," not an "artist," I said "screw it" and let it be.

The drawing, which to this day is infantile and nonprofessional, received lots of comments. Dozens of people came up to me later and told me how much they liked it. The only thing I can figure is that it demonstrated my vulnerability. It opened the curtain to a piece of me.

48

But the point is I wasn't capable of judging what "art" was good or bad. Or rather I wasn't able to judge what bad art (yes, it was bad) might do for someone else, how it might move someone, how it might need to be said.

If we always judge, we cut things off before they get a chance to really live. I don't know if you've ever spent any time at a hospital nursery, but babies don't alway look so good when they're first born. It's a good thing we don't judge them and say, "Uh-uh! Reject pile."

You've got to be willing to be vulnerable. To give up any investment in what the neighbors think.

This may come as a big surprise, but even the most renowned artists make messes. As Anne Lamott says, "We all feel like we're pulling teeth. Even for the best of writers, the right words and sentences do not come flowing out like ticker tape."

The trick, she says, is to get something . . . *anything* . . . down.

She calls it writing "shitty first drafts." If you write lots of terrible first drafts, "You'd learn that good second drafts can spring from these, and you'd see that big sloppy imperfect messes have value."

Messes, like compost piles, are fertile, brimming, and beating with life.

Last year, an unidentified nonflying vine sprouted from my compost pile. For months, I watched it wind around the garden, eagerly awaiting its first blossom, wondering what vegetable I'd inadvertently planted. Finally, it appeared, green and spotty. I assumed it was a zucchini.

One morning, I plucked it from the vine to make zucchini bread. My neighbor, who was outside hosing down her two-year-old, said, "Wow! What a pumpkin."

So, no, I didn't get zucchini bread. But I got one of the best jack-o'-lantern pumpkins in the neighborhood.

The point is, we don't know. We just have to show up and do the work.

WRITE A SKETCH FOR
SATURDAY NIGHT LIVE

Lorne Michaels, Are You Watching?

When I was a kid, *Laugh-In* was the hottest show on TV. My friends and I used to write *Laugh-In* skits and perform them for our parents. I played Edith Ann and that crazy telephone operator ("one ringy-dingy") who stuffed Kleenex down her bra, and you can bet your sweet bippie we gave out Fickle Fingers of Fate.

Now if we could do this while we were in seventh grade, surely you can do it now.

Your task this week is to write a sketch that could appear on *Saturday Night Live.* Maybe you'll even invite your friends to make one up too, and stage your own *Saturday Night Live.*

"Schwing!"   Bass-O-Matic

"Yeah, that's the ticket!"

Samurai Night Fever "Ooooh Noooooooo..."

"Land Shark"   # Emily Litella

"We are two wild and crazy guys."

Babwa Wawa

The Judy Miller Show

E. Buzz Miller's Animal Kingdom

More Fun Stuff

Make yourself a pair of angel wings.

Find and read three poems by Rumi.

Eat lunch somewhere unusual—in a tree,
at a homeless center.

You're in Good Company

"I suffer as always from the fear of putting down
the first line. It is amazing the terrors, the magic,
the prayers, the straightening shyness that assails
one," said John Steinbeck.

Week Nine

> If your heart is pulling you in a direction that has
> mystery and wonder, trust it and follow it.
>
> **DAVID WILCOX**

YA GOTTA BELIEVE

In January 1959, a thirty-year-old eighth-grade dropout from Detroit borrowed $800 from a family savings plan to buy a house, not an unusual goal for a man of his age. Only this enterprising thirty-year-old had his sights set a little higher. He was going to use that unassuming two-story house to start a record company.

The man, of course, is Berry Gordy, the record company is Motown, and the plan—well, let's just say that it worked. Between 1959 and 1972, Gordy's Motown released 535 singles, 75 percent of which made the pop charts. From a recording studio barely larger than a king-size bed, Gordy produced sixty number-one hits before he moved to Hollywood and sold Motown to MCA Records for $61 million.

I tell you this story because it demonstrates the power of opening to a bigger possibility. Berry Gordy could have easily settled for less. He was black at a time when black wasn't yet beautiful. He dropped out of school in eighth grade, had already failed at an upstart boxing career, and could neither play an instrument nor read music.

But he had a dream. He wanted to write songs. And if nobody else would produce them, well, he'd just do it himself.

Catching a dream is the point at which all of us must start. We see a vision. We hear a tapping on our heart. We start to wonder if "maybe, just maybe, we might be able to" . . . write a song, dance a poem, leap into a new way of being. We become willing to say "It *is* possible."

But not even Gordy could have known that when he recruited nineteen-year-old Smokey Robinson and his high school quartet, the Matadors (later to become the Miracles), he was launching one of the biggest musical phenomena of our times.

When we first begin to listen to our dreams, we don't always know where they're leading us. This is good news. If we could see the final outcome, we might get scared off, put on the brakes, think, "Whoa, Nelly, that's way too big for me." So luckily all we have to do for now is take that first step, put that first toe out the door.

The other thing that the Motown phenomenon demonstrates is the wealth of talent that so often goes undiscovered. Had Berry Gordy been content to plug lugnuts at a Detroit auto plant, one of many jobs he tried before starting Motown, he would have never plucked Diana Ross, Stevie Wonder, and hundreds of other poor black kids out of the ghetto. It seems impossible that superstars of their stature might have taken another path. But had Diana Ross not caught a vision, she could very well be just another bag lady on 9th Street; Stevie Wonder, another blind kid on welfare. Thank God they had the opportunity to tap the creative spirit that was within them.

If Gordy hadn't turned 2648 West Grand Boulevard into a "happening" place to be, "Heard It Through the Grapevine,"

53

"Ain't No Mountain High Enough," "I'll Be There," and thousands of other songs would never have been written.

I, for one, would have had a completely different upbringing. If it wasn't for the Four Tops hit "Reach Out I'll Be There," I'd have never danced with Andy Gilmore at Jim Rinklemeyer's party. I'd have never known he wore Brut cologne, never known he smelled like mothballs—a discovery that can undoubtedly be traced to the tweed jacket he'd stolen from his older brother's closet—and never known how it felt to be thirteen and helplessly smitten. Unfortunately, I lacked the nerve to ever speak to him again.

How many of us lack the nerve to investigate the creative spirit within us? How many of us are on spiritual "welfare" because we haven't caught the vision? The same kind of talent that Gordy found in his ghetto protégés is hidden in the people we walk by every day. It lays hidden because nobody bothered to look, nobody bothered to say, "Hey, look what we can do." It lies hidden behind thoughts of unworthiness, behind "masks" that we put on for a good show.

Each and every one of us has that same creative spirit. But, no, you're probably thinking Detroit was different. The list of superstars goes on and on—the Temps, the Tops, the Vandellas, the Supremes. But you know what? Gordy could have just as easily opened that record company and been just as successful in Cleveland or Chicago or Omaha, Nebraska, for that matter. There are Temps, Tops, Vandellas, and Supremes everywhere. There are people that are just as talented, just as musical. The only thing they don't have is Gordy's vision.

This is not to deny the huge talent that existed in Detroit at that time. What they did on that little three-track recording system in Studio A can only be described as the musical equivalent of sitting in the front of the bus.

But it only happened because one man was willing to step up to the plate, was willing to say, "I believe."

54

MAKE A SELF-PORTRAIT

Smile, You're on *Candid Camera*

When I made mine, I went to a photo booth—you know, those places you find at the mall where you put in a buck and get three poses of yourself. I went in with hats and different costumes (not that I had time to really change them between poses) and made faces.

I blew them up on a copy machine, added graphics and photos, and came up with what I believe was a unique self-portrait.

And remember, Frida Kahlo made a whole career out of painting nothing but her own self-portrait.

Create a new kind of pie.

Come up with a new Constitutional amendment.

Design a treehouse.

You're in Good Company

After Fred Astaire's first screen test, the memo from the testing director of MGM, dated 1933, said, "Can't act. Slightly bald, can dance a little." Astaire hung that memo over the fireplace in his Beverly Hills home.

WEEK 10

DEMYSTIFYING THE ARTIST

Natalie Goldberg, poet, painter, and Zen Buddhist, was recently interviewed by *Sounds True Catalog*, a quarterly catalog that offers, as they put it, "audios and videos for the inner life." One of their new offerings is a six-cassette package of Goldberg reading her classic *Writing Down the Bones*, an inspiring book about writing practice.

The interviewer asks her about talent and she says, "I guess I don't believe in talent. I know talent exists. Like maybe you're born pretty—but so what? What does that get you?"

She goes on to say that talent, to her, is like a water table under the earth. You tap into it with your effort and it flows through you. It's equally available to everyone.

When someone decides to dig for oil, nobody questions whether or not they have the "proper talent." The oil is down

57

there. It doesn't care who gets it. It isn't thinking, "Well, I like Bunker F. Hunt more than Pam Grout, so I think I'll wait to spring up for him." It's there for anybody who has the desire to keep digging. Nobody needs to see your degree, nobody cares if you have formal training.

Granted, some of us live in Oklahoma or Texas or, say, Saudi Arabia, where every other acre has a potential oil well, but what's to stop any one of us from moving there and buying a shovel?

So the good news is anybody who wants to be an artist can be. All it takes is (a) the desire and (b) the willingness to keep digging. And unlike oil, which is predicted to eventually run out, there are no limits on creativity. In fact, the more you use it, the more you get.

But the important point is you are tapping into something else. You are being a channel. And that's really all it is.

Anne Lamott calls herself "the designated typist."

"It's like the characters have really bad handwriting, so it's up to me to get it all down," she says.

Those who bite their fingernails to the quick, worrying that they're not "talented" enough (yes, that means all of us) have it all wrong. Do you actually think you're the one creating this stuff?

Henry Miller, the famous writer and painter, says that any artist who really understood himself would be very humble.

"He would recognize himself as a man who has a certain faculty which he was destined to use for the service of others. He has nothing to be proud of, his name means nothing, he's only an instrument in a long procession."

Faulkner once said that if he hadn't written *The Sound and the Fury*, *Absalom, Absalom!*, *Requiem for a Nun*, and other books we now regard as classics, someone else would have written them.

Ideas and inventions and messages are floating around in the universe, seeking life. It doesn't matter who gives it to them. Like airplanes, they need places to land. Our job is to be the air traffic controllers who steer them in.

That's why in 1858, when Charles Darwin was writing his startling, groundbreaking, never-before-heard theory of evolution, he got a letter from an Alfred Russel Wallace, who basically said the same thing. That's why Isaac Newton and Gottfried Leibniz invented calculus at the same time, why Henry Ford and that guy in Germany came up with automobiles in approximately the same year. The consciousness was right for those creations, and Darwin, Newton, and Ford were willing to spend the time and the energy to write them down, to give them a voice.

In 1836, long before scientists had instruments to study outer space, astronomers in Jonathan Swift's *Gulliver's Travels* reported that Mars had two moons. How could he have known this? In 1898, M. F. Mansfield wrote a novel about a fabulous Atlantic ocean liner named the *Titan*. Sailing with the rich and famous, it hit an iceberg and sank. And like the similar-named boat that sailed eighteen years later, it didn't have enough lifeboats.

Was Mansfield a seer, a psychic—or was he just plugged into that mystery that's available to all of us?

The reason we idolize and canonize our artists is because they're transcribing important stuff. But they, the artists, are not the geniuses. The genius is the incredible stuff that's out there in the ethers. Their genius is that they were willing to transcribe.

"The idea that I created this piece of music is kind of pompous," says Keith Richards of the Rolling Stones. "Music is everywhere: All you've got to do is pick it up. It's like being a receiver."

Eudora Welty once called her publisher after getting galleys because she couldn't remember writing a certain passage. The editor picked up her original typewritten manuscript and read back that passage word for word.

Author Delta Wedding said it was as if she were taken on board an alien spacecraft to write, then returned to her desk with no memory of where she'd been or what she'd been doing.

"People get married and I didn't even realize they were engaged. They die and I'm surprised," said Pat Conroy of the characters in his novels. "They take on this subterranean life of their own."

In other words, we are channeling something bigger than our mortal talent, tapping into something greater.

Until recently, *channeling* was a term associated with palm readers and fortune tellers, snake-charmer types who might be fun to visit with a cast of girlfriends during a bachelorette party, but nobody to take seriously.

Yet, many of us accept the story of the Bible being channeled and call what came through Matthew, Mark, Luke, and John "the word of God." What makes us think God quit talking in 15 B.C., when the Bible first went into print?

We're channels, people. Nothing more.

Remember the Ouija boards we played with as kids? Back when we wanted to know who we were going to marry or whether or not Billy McDaniels even knew we were alive?

That's all it really takes. Put your fingertips gently on the plastic divining rod. Say a prayer. And begin.

WRITE A 1,000-WORD AUTOBIOGRAPHY.

Life 101

That's four double-spaced pages, not a daunting assignment. Except that you've got to really look at your life and decide what's important, what shaped you. What are the events that took you to this place in your life?

More Fun Stuff

Write five fortunes you'd like to find in a fortune cookie.

Stage *The Newlywed Game* at home with three couples.

Write five questions for Trivial Pursuit.

You're in Good Company

An agent refused to circulate Tony Hillerman's first Navajo-based mystery for fear it would ruin her reputation.

W E E K 1 1

I want you to foam at the mouth and wander into unknown fields.

NATALIE GOLDBERG

THE REAL GIFTS OF CREATIVITY

Most people have it wrong. They think the reason they want to write a book or a movie, to act or to dance is because they want to be Matthew McConaughey or Joyce Carol Oates. They want to be on *Oprah*.

They assume the fruit of creativity is seeing their name on *The New York Times* best-seller list or winning a gold statue named Oscar. Money, fame, and fans, they're just sure, are the presents under the creativity Christmas tree.

Don't get me wrong. Those gifts are nice. And they certainly might come. Like Keith Richards of the Rolling Stones says, "People have the need to set people above themselves—like gods. In lieu of finding what the greater power is, they set up their own earthly version. I stand on the stage and I think, 'What are you looking at me for, a damned old junkie hacking away at the guitar?'"

Yes, many people make millions of dollars on their art. Sometimes there's so much fame and so many fans that the only way to travel is incognito.

But that isn't the gift.

Author Anne Lamott describes fame as a plate of cocaine. It certainly feels good for a while. It takes your mind off your everyday existence. But when it's all over (say in three weeks, when you're bumped off the best-seller list by the next weight-loss book), you're crazy again, searching desperately for that next fix, that next shot of fame.

Getting on a best-seller list does not a happy artist make. True gifts are those that rock lives, shake things up, and transform us. Getting a big advance might get you a new car or a ticket to the country club. But it won't crack open your heart or deepen your soul.

The real gifts will. The true gifts of creativity are the writing, the painting, the acting. The doing. It's the journey, always the journey, that bears fruit.

Singer-songwriter Iris DeMent describes the creative process as having your own personal hankie. "Music came along and provided me a means of working things out," she explained.

Art gives us a forum for things that are rotting inside us. All of us hold on to a lot of emotional garbage. We guard it selfishly, like a baby grasping its rattle. We're programmed at an early age to "keep quiet," so this stuff just stays inside of us, smoldering like ashes. These ashes, these unhealed places rest in our body and play hide-and-seek until we end up depressed and physically sick.

The place to put it is in a story or a painting or a poem. If you stick with your art, you'll be surprised at the freedom you will eventually gain. Serving an art fulfills our deepest needs to be heard, to be visible, to shout a holy "yes" to the miraculous that's every day around us.

Serving an art makes you feel alive, to pulse with expansive energy. Without it, we shrink like the wicked witch from *The Wizard of Oz* after Dorothy throws water on her.

Art opens our eyes.

It burns through the fog. It makes you notice things. Things that matter, like the drop of dew that's about to spill off the tip of a chrysanthemum, a shooting star, the lady in the green hat who pushes her grocery cart to the bowling alley every afternoon at 3 P.M.

You'll notice you live in a great big world that's rich with details, abundant with beauty.

Once you start to notice these things, what step could be next but saying "thank you"? What possible emotion could anyone who really sees ever have but gratitude? Until we commit to being conscious, which is another way of saying being committed to our creativity, we ignore life's beauty and richness. We have so many blessings, yet we walk by them every day.

As someone once said about Jesus putting clay on the blind man's eye: It's not hard to make men see. The challenge is making them *see*.

How many of us are like that blind man, blind to our own beauty, blind to the wide, deep galaxies within us?

MAKE A BALLOON SCULPTURE

Not Just a Lot of Hot Air

Bag of balloons? $1.25. Your own hot air? Free.

A little twist here, a little twist there and you can make dogs and cats and even hats.

While this might sound frivolous, hardly worth your precious time, dig this: I just met a husband-and-wife team who make a respectable living making balloon sculptures at festivals and special events. And they've turned it into an art. I watched them twist everything from Ariel the Little Mermaid to Elvis Presley complete with black pompadour and gold lamé jumpsuit.

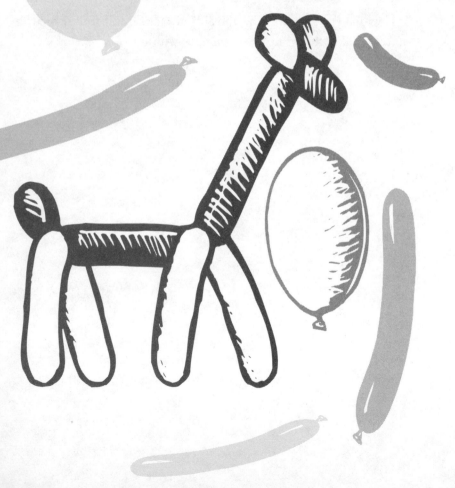

Call the most creative person you know and find out what they're doing. It will inspire you.

Learn two homeopathic remedies.

Make six kinds of applesauce.

You're in Good Company

Even the great Don Henley is not immune to self-doubt. He says, "Who am I to be doing this? Why do I deserve to get my feelings and opinions on this blank piece of vinyl that a million people are going to hear? Always, I must overcome those feelings of inadequacy, those feelings of 'I don't deserve this.'"

Week 12

Don't stop biting your fingernails. Just stop biting one.

SONNY KRASNER

BABY STEPS

And now for my first number . . .

When we sit down to tackle our first project, most of us have something in mind like winning a Grammy award or painting the next *Mona Lisa*. But this is like trying to swim the Atlantic.

You're bound to run into tidal waves and icebergs, your muscles are going to get sore, and you're probably going to give up before you get to Bermuda. It might be better to begin with the swimming pool in the backyard.

This week, we're going to talk about something you mastered in kindergarten. Remember "Mother, May I"? Remember baby steps?

Those tiny, two-inch shuffles got you to the finish line just as effectively as bunny hops, scissors steps, or what you really thought you wanted—giant steps.

Jan Steward, when writing her first book, was feeling overwhelmed until a friend dropped by with a beadwork piece from India. It was ten inches wide and thirty feet long, and it illustrated a complicated love story complete with courtship, wedding, and

68

the final escape from both lovers' families. It was made from beads the size of sesame seeds.

Steward took one look at it and asked, "How on earth could a person ever do this?"

Her friend rubbed his chin thoughtfully and answered, "Well, I think first you take a white bead . . ."

All you have to do for today is take that first white bead. Make one little baby step in the direction of your dream. It doesn't have to be huge; maybe it's writing a description of your character's hot pink negligee or drawing a quick sketch of one daffodil in your painting. Don't even think about what the character might say to her mother when she walks in with a bag of groceries or about that pregnant bumblebee buzzing around the flower.

For now, writing about the character's negligee is enough. Give that negligee everything you've got. The rest, for the time being, doesn't matter.

Anne Lamott passes out one-inch picture frames in her writing classes to remind students that all they have to do is write what they can see in that tiny, barely there frame.

If you do it any other way, you're gonna drown. You're going to hit that first iceberg, throw up your hands, and say, "I quit." Writing a novel or sculpting an angel is overwhelming. It's like handing over every one of your deepest needs to the guy with his picture in the post office. It's huge, really more than any human being can be expected to take on.

But by taking it bead by bead, day after day, you can get clear across the Atlantic. Put a few beads on every day—put them on like you might practice scales on a piano. Do it as a debt of honor.

It's this daily "beadwork" that builds muscles. Just like the weight lifter who bulks up his triceps and biceps by pumping iron day after day, you're developing your creative muscle—the stamina, the sense of honor that will get you across the Atlantic.

It's important to see these tiny steps as tools, to think of yourself as a carpenter or a cement layer. Trying to be an "artist" is

69

enough to freeze anyone. Trying to make something that will be admired for centuries is enough to stop a bull charging for a red cape.

When Barbara Walters interviewed Sir Laurence Olivier, she asked him how he wanted to be remembered.

"As a workman," he replied.

She was surprised. "Don't you want us to think of you as an actor or an artist?"

"No," he went on, "that doesn't matter. Shakespeare was a workman, poets are workmen. God is a workman and that is how I wish to be remembered."

So put on your overalls, tie up your boots, and mount that first rung of the ladder. Step by step. It'll take you all the way to the stars.

WRITE TITLES FOR FIVE COUNTRY-AND-WESTERN SONGS

Yee-haw!

This week you are going to be a country-and-western songwriter. It doesn't matter if you've never written a song. This week, you have permission to write a really awful country-and-western song. Or maybe a good one. Sometimes when we give ourselves permission to do things poorly, brilliance surfaces.

Your job is to come up with either one song or at least five country-and-western song titles. Remember, they're often funny and usually involve heartbreak, mommas, and trucks. Here are some that have actually made it to the C&W charts:

- ✪ "If I Said You Have a Beautiful Body Would You Hold It Against Me?"

- ✪ "I'm So Miserable It's Almost Like You Were Here"

- ✪ "My John Deere Was Breaking Your Fields While Your Dear John Was Breaking My Heart"

- ✪ "I Don't Know Whether to Kill Myself or Go Bowling"

- ✪ "She Got the Goldmine (I Got the Shaft)"

More Fun Stuff

Spend two hours in a hammock doing nothing.

Rent a camcorder and tape yourself acting out a scene from *It's a Wonderful Life*.

Find the best vantage point possible and watch the sunset.

You're in Good Company

Isabel Allende had to publish three novels before she felt comfortable putting "writer" rather than "housewife" in the space for "occupation" when filling out a form. *Writer* was such a big word, she explained.

SUMMONING THE ANGELS

The trick for luring the muses is pretty simple.

Show up.

It you want to write or paint or make a film, you've got to set a time and be there—every morning or every evening or every lunch hour.

The muses will let you set your own hours, but you've got to set the hours. You've got to convince them that you're serious. Dreaming about writing a book will not get the book written. Reading books about painting will not get the painting painted. You have to take action.

Look at it from the muses' point of view. If you had an important project to give to the world, would you pick some two-timing, tap-dancing Willy, someone who was too scared to make the commitment? No, you'd pick the person who showed up every day, rain or shine. You'd nominate the person who was loyal, who was like the dog in the backyard, always ready with his tongue hanging out.

Week Thirteen

This may not sound like a pretty proposition, but if you think about it, it's exciting news. It takes the onus off of having to possess this great talent. Isn't that what we're all afraid of? That we're not as good as Toni Morrison, as pretty as Michelle Pfeiffer. We know it. Our friends and family know it. But do we really want to hang it all out for the world to know it, too?

When I read anything by Pat Conroy, I feel about two inches tall. I want to hide, to take any reference to "writer" off my résumé. Two days ago, I finished *Divine Secrets of the Ya-Ya Sisterhood* by Rebecca Wells. That book was so beautifully written, I was tempted to throw in the towel. Compared to her, I'm a neophyte, a plebeian nobody.

Well, that isn't the point. Part of the reason those writers perform with such eloquence is because they've put in the time. They've practiced over and over again.

They've been there through thick and thin. They've written every day when there were other things they could have been doing. They've written when it wasn't convenient, when they felt like they didn't measure up, when they thought they were as talented as sewer slime. They convinced their muses they were loyal devotees.

The good part of this equation is it takes away the need to worry about anything but being a good dog. The only quality you need is loyalty. Nothing else.

In music, it's pretty obvious to see the connection between genius and time spent. Let's say the muse has this great piece of music. She has two candidates—the guy who bought a guitar three months ago but still hasn't picked it up or the guy who has been practicing every day for ten years—the guy who practiced his scales, who kept going even when he sounded like a garbage disposal. It doesn't take a genius to figure out that the muse has little choice but to go with the guy with the technical ability to play the masterpiece she wants to give.

As John Irving says, "The only thing that gets it done is doing the same thing seven or eight hours a day, for two or three years and getting better at it all the time."

There are thousands of talented nobodies. As John Gardner says, "Genius is as common as old shoes."

The muses have little choice but to go with loyalty.

Lawrence Block tells the story of a wannabe writer who somehow convinced him to read his novel. He said it was so bad that he wanted to plug his nose and hold it out with two fingers. Rather than discourage the guy, however, he told him it needed some work, but to keep trying. Block said that any other critic would have suggested this guy quickly commence on a different career path. Definitely no need to quit his day job. Two years later, the same guy comes back with a different novel, a new offering. The same guy who showed nary an inkling of talent now has this masterpiece. Who would have thought?

Nobody on this earth. But the angels in heaven were smiling.

Madeleine L'Engle once wrote about a small village in Bavaria. When the village clock maker died, leaving no children or apprentices, all the clocks and the watches of the village eventually, over time, broke down. Years later, a renowned clock maker showed up, and all the people rushed to him, begging him to fix their broken-down timepieces. The wise old clock maker, who had only so much time, looked at the many abandoned timepieces and finally announced that he would fix only the ones that had been kept wound. They were the only ones, he said, that would be able to remember how to keep time.

We may not be able to make our clocks run perfectly, but at least we can get up every day and wind our clocks so they won't forget.

INVENT A NEW SANDWICH

Move Over, Dagwood!

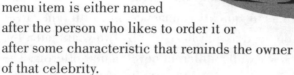

There's a deli in New York
City that sells Woody
Allens and Burt
Reynoldses and many
other sandwiches named
for famous people. Each
menu item is either named
after the person who likes to order it or
after some characteristic that reminds the owner
of that celebrity.

Luckily, you don't have to make it to Broadway to have your
own sandwich. In fact, all it takes is a little imagination and the
willingness to try some new combinations.

One woman who loved sweet potatoes and bean sprouts created
her own sandwich with sweet potatoes and bean sprouts. Maybe
you have a favorite bread? Or you want to use the sensational
cranberry nut bread you make in your own breadmaker.
Remember, be outrageous, be
original, have fun.

Take your sketchbook to the park.

Invent a toy you wanted as a kid.

Send yourself a postcard.

You're in Good Company

Roy Lichtenstein launched his art career by drawing Mickey Mouse cartoons for his kids.

Never ask whether you can do something.
Say instead that you are doing it. Then fasten your seatbelts.

JULIA CAMERON

INNER WILD CHILD

There has been a huge movement over the last decade to get in touch with the "inner child." She's become our best friend, our most trusted confidante. The only problem is we've spent so much time getting her to talk about her father that was never there for her and the day-care worker that locked her in the closet that we forgot to ask her about the tea party with the fairy king.

Kids know important things—things we "mature grown-ups" have forgotten. Kids know that mud puddles are for sailing sticks across, that snowstorms are for making angels, and that broken broomsticks are really prancing ponies. They know M&M's are better than money and that finding a pretty seashell is an important way to spend the day.

And when it comes to making art, it never even occurs to a first grader that he might not know how to paint, how to dance, how to sculpt. After all, Play-Doh can be made into anything. Kids know how to dream big dreams, how to make friends with dragons and princes and elves.

This is the inner child we want to consult.

Not only do we want to call back that inner wild child, the one that climbs trees and builds sand castles, but we want to do the things kids do.

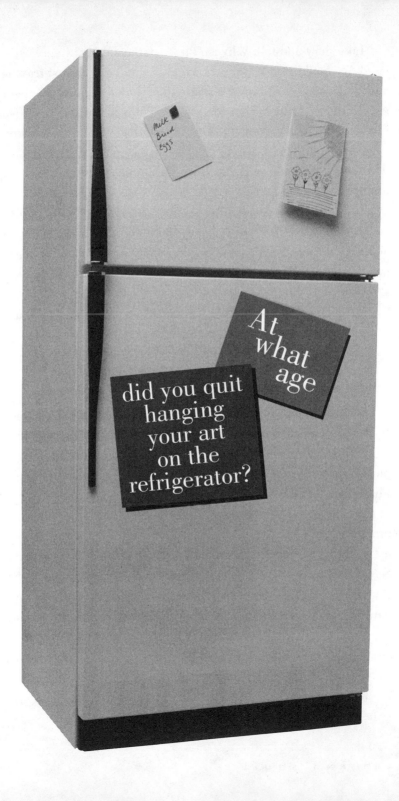

Like show-and-tell. Why isn't this a normal thing? Every week or so we should get together with families and our closest friends and show them something we really like, something unique about us. We should bring in some doodle we made on the side of a Visa bill or something we thought up while waiting at the dry cleaners.

Adults still think things up. We just don't tell anyone. We don't think it's important. Not with lawns that need mowing and mufflers that need fixing.

How much closer we'd all be if we stopped long enough to honor one another in a circle of show-and-tell. If we listened to one another's stories, looked at each other's creations. We're all hungry for community. We need more ways to connect. Adults still need show-and-tell. Literally.

We also still need story time, music time, nap time, and snack time. Probably even more than kids.

I'm always envious of Tasman's music classes. She gets to play the tambourine, sing silly songs, and dance in wild circles while I watch from the sidelines as a proper mom.

Whatever happened to hanging fingerpaints on our refrigerator? Whatever happened to giving book reports? Playing charades?

My highest vision for *Art and Soul* is that communities of people would form circles to do these projects together, that they would form what Julia Cameron calls "sacred circles."

But instead of working on all the "inner child" work that was probably necessary when *The Artist's Way* first came out, I see them getting together to show off their self-portraits, their *Art and Soul* badges, their balloon sculptures. I see them laughing at the various adventures of leaving poems on sidewalks and spray-painting grand statements on bridges. I see a big potluck with everyone sampling the staggering variety of sandwiches they created. I see celebrations of the holidays they made up, variety shows with skits and made-up instruments.

But most of all, I see healing and fun—life as it was for a six-year-old.

CREATE A CHARACTER

What a Character!

Your job this week is to create a character. When screenwriters write movies they have to create characters that seem real. Once you have a character that meets another character your movie is practically written.

Tell us everything about your character. What does he like for breakfast? Has she ever been married? What did her parents do? What is her favorite song? Where does he work? Pick a name and just start writing.

Here's an example:

I.ydia is forty-two years old.

Lydia is single and lonely.

Lydia's favorite cereal is Cap'n Crunch.

Lydia once had a job painting tennis shoes.

Lydia has had three homosexual experiences in her life but tells herself they don't count because she was drunk at the time.

Lydia has glasses but rarely wears them.

Lydia has an older brother she has never been able to get along with.

Lydia has an intuitive ability to predict anyone's future.

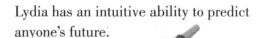

More Fun Stuff

Write a new ending to a mystery novel.

Impersonate your favorite cartoon character.

Host a Barbra Streisand or Keanu Reeves film festival.

You're in Good Company

Tom Wolfe says, "The awful thing about the first sentence of any book is that as soon as you've written it you realize this piece of work is not going to be the great thing that you envision. It can't be."

He was a bold man
that first ate an oyster. **JONATHAN SWIFT**

LISTENING TO
YOUR OWN VOICE

When Walt Disney was in grade school, a well-meaning teacher, peering over at the flowers he was scribbling in the margins of his paper, tapped him on the shoulder and said, "Walt, honey, those flowers are nice, but flowers don't have faces."

Walt turned around, looked her straight in the eye, and pronounced boldly, "Mine do."

This is the confidence with which we must create.

We must refuse to listen to anything or anybody except the inner urgings of our soul. Very early on, we turn over the reins to something outside ourselves. The coach tells us if we're good enough to be on the basketball team. The music teacher tells us if we have the talent to sing in the choir. Our teachers give us arbitrary grades that tell us if we're smart enough to make the honor roll, bright enough to get into college.

Our art teachers give us the rules: Grass is green, skies are blue, and flowers do not have faces.

Robert Fulghum's now-famous essay *All I Really Need to Know I Learned in Kindergarten* was recently made into a stage play. In one of the first scenes, the kindergarten teacher asks her fresh young students how many of them are dancers.

"I am! I am!" they all shout exuberantly.

"And how many of you are singers?" she continues.

Again, all of them wave their hands wildly.

"Painters?"

Unanimous hand-waving.

"Writers?"

More unanimous hand-waving.

In fourth grade, another teacher asks the same questions of the same students. Now only a third of the students are dancers, singers, painters, writers.

By high school, the number who are willing to claim artistic talent is down to a paltry handful. Where did the confidence and enthusiasm go?

Some well-meaning parent or teacher probably told them they were not painters. Some aptitude test with a fancy title gave an official score that said they had better give up that misguided ambition to be a writer. Try accounting. Some guidance counselor broke the news that only a chosen few have artistic talent.

Why did we listen?

How can anybody else know what color your flowers are? How can anybody else know what notes you're supposed to sing?

In a book called *Musicians in Tune,* Jenny Boyd, former wife of Mick Fleetwood, interviewed seventy-five contemporary musicians—everyone from Eric Clapton to Branford Marsalis. What she found was that many of today's successful musicians were outsiders, not part of the "in" crowd in high school. This alienation forced them to listen to that inner voice, the one that so often gets crowded out. Out of desperation and a sense of not belonging, they were forced to call upon their own resources.

They held on to their power to decide whether or not their flowers had faces.

You are God. You have the ability to paint, to write, to dance. What comes out of you is holy. What you have to say is magic. Throw off the shackles of those well-meaning parents, those misguided teachers.

They know what's right for them. But they haven't a clue in Anchorage what is right for you.

Only you know that.

And you do know. You don't need another workshop, another book, another psychic reading. Bring it forth.

As for Walt Disney, well, his flowers certainly did have faces. In *Alice in Wonderland*, his eighteenth animated feature, the flowers not only had faces, but they had voices, opinions, and a chorus that entertained Alice with the whimsical song "All in the Golden Afternoon."

If you really have to listen to somebody outside yourself, try Frank Zappa, who says anybody can be a composer. After all, he says, "A composer is just a guy who goes around forcing his will on unsuspecting air molecules."

Here are his simple instructions:

1. Declare your *intention* to create a "composition."

2. *Start* a piece at some time.

3. *Cause something to happen* over a period of time. (It doesn't matter what happens in your "time hole"—we have critics to tell us whether it's any good or not, so we won't worry about that part.)

(continued on next page)

(continued from previous page)

4. *End the piece at some time* (or keep it going, telling the audience it is a "work in progress").

5. Get a part-time job so you can continue to do stuff like this.

He goes on to say that the most important thing in art is the frame.

"For painting: literally; for other arts: figuratively—because, without this humble appliance, you can't know where *The Art* stops and *The Real World* begins.

"You have to put a 'box' around it because otherwise, what is that shit on the wall?"

He said that if a famous musician decides to put a contact microphone on his throat and drink carrot juice, then that gurgling qualifies as his composition because he put a frame around it and said so. "Take it or leave it. I now will this to be music."

After that it's just a matter of taste. Anything can be music, but it doesn't become music until someone wills it to be music, and the audience listening to it decides to perceive it as music.

LEAVE YOUR PERSONAL STATEMENT SOMEWHERE

Sweet Graffit

Yes, that means graffiti. You can use a can of spray
paint. Chalk will do. But the biggest part of this
assignment is coming up with your statement.
What do you need to tell the world? What do you
know that needs to be said? Find a good place
(the bus station, the sidewalk outside the grocery store)
and go when no one is watching.

More Fun Stuff

Do a Polaroid study of mall rats.

Rent a Pink Panther video.

Eat two desserts naked.

You're in Good Company

Pulitzer Prize–winning poet Anne Sexton was too scared to call about taking her first poetry class. A friend had to call and sign her up.

Make Art, Not War

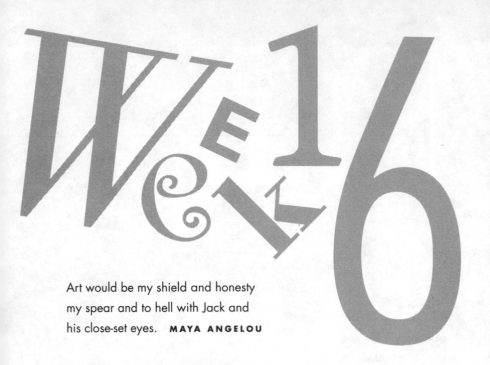

WEEK 16

Art would be my shield and honesty my spear and to hell with Jack and his close-set eyes. **MAYA ANGELOU**

OPEN SESAME

I may not know what color car you drive or what kind of grades you got in high school. But there's one thing I *do* know about you. Your deepest desire is to be close to people, to give and receive love. To use a term that the media has beaten to death, you long to have intimacy.

The reason I know this is because it is my greatest desire, your Great-Aunt Edna's (yes, the same Aunt Edna that is always complaining about your skirts being too short) greatest desire, and the desire of every human who ever walked this great round earth. We all want to connect, to be close.

Lately, however, we've gotten really good at connecting through what medical intuitive Carolyn Myss calls "woundology." Here's how it works. I want to get to know you. I ask where you're from, tell you I'm from Kansas City. We talk for a few minutes about the museum I might have heard about in your hometown, you ask me about the famous barbecue restaurant in Kansas City. End of conversation. Next, I ask what you do, tell you I'm a writer. I say, "Wow, I always admired people who were teachers or plumbers or whatever it is you do." You say something about always wanting to write. Or about a friend in grade school who published a story in *Ladies' Home Journal*. Again, end of conversation. However, if I happen to tell you that my dad wasn't there for me, that I used to date an alcoholic, and that I'm still a recovering codependent, boy, do we have a landslide of conversation.

Only problem is that from now on, we'll have to deal with each other with kid gloves. Don't stand me up because then I'll be reminded of my dad and I'll have to be really sad and reject you and blah, blah, blah, blah, blah.

Yeah, we're connected all right, but is it the kind of connection that really serves us, that really nurtures a friendship?

As Myss points out, these twelve-step groups, which are very therapeutic and extremely helpful for finally owning your past, are meant to be a bridge. They're simply a temporary life raft for getting to the other side. We don't have to swim around in the muck and mire forever.

What I'd like to propose is an even better way to connect. Let's tell each other our deepest dreams. Let's read each other the poems we've secretly written. Let's pretend that you're Tom Cruise and I'm Nicole Kidman and let's go out and chow strawberry shortcake.

Sure, we're still going to have anger, angst, and depression, but if we channel those burning emotions into a character, a short story, a song, we find that we can let it go. We've made it into something, something that's tangible and real, something we can share with another human being. Talking about a problem is fine. Everyone needs to feel that someone cares, that someone is listening. But when you turn your depression into something—a story, a poem—it becomes concrete and you suddenly own it instead of it owning you.

I go to a group on the second Wednesday of every month. Although the title changes every six months or so when Bob, the white-haired sage who leads the group, puts a description in the local free university catalog, its basic purpose is always the same. We share what we've created. For three, sometimes more, hours, we get together and share the headlines of our hearts. Jesse reads a poem about faith or shows a painting of an angel that he's working on. Bart plays his banjo or tells a story about a wounded owl that he found at the edge of his farm. Connie reads a love sonnet to her daughter. Lois shows a detailed drawing of a feather that she drew on the back of a postcard. I read my favorite children's story or share a travel article about a voyage I took to the Galápagos Islands.

We share our hearts. We share the inner stirrings of our soul. We share things that normally stay bottled up inside people.

Yeah, we're all different. We're black, white, gay, straight, male, female, old, and young. But I tell you what, I have never felt closer to a group of people—anywhere. We connect on a level that's much higher—our God-selves are dancing, if you will. Yeah, we suffer health problems and relationship issues and all the other stuff that goes with being human. But when Bob starts reciting a poem or when Joannes gets out his latest piece of pottery, that stuff means about as much as a stock quote from 1959.

We soar.

There are probably a million ways to connect with another human being. And in forty-two years of living, I've probably tried them all. But I now know that the most intimate, the most nurturing for me and for my confidants is the connection of the spirit. I'm tired of living in the gutter, sick of leading with all my weaknesses, hoping that maybe you'll like me because I'm insecure or scared. Yeah, I've thought about taking a razor blade to my arm. I've also gotten down on my hands and knees and begged a man not to leave me. But I'm also a dancing goddess, a twirling master who longs to dance with the God in you.

MAKE YOUR OWN STATIONERY

Dear John

You can paint it, cut it, paste dried grasses to shopping bags. Just make something that represents the voice you want to offer the world. If you really feel ambitious and want to make your own paper, check out *Tonia Todman's Paper-Making Book*.

Hug fourteen people.

Rent your favorite Disney cartoon and eat
gummy worms.

Camp out in the backyard.

You're in Good Company

Says Maya Angelou, "Every time I write a book,
every time I face that yellow pad, the challenge is
so great. I have written eleven books, but each
time I think, 'Oh, they're going to find out now. I've
run a game on everybody and they're going to find
me out.'"

WEEK 21

The salvation you have been seeking elsewhere has already arrived,
woven into the very warp and woof of your innermost self.

BOB SAVINO

EASY OR HARD: YOU DECIDE

This week, we'll endeavor to overcome the misconception that
doing art is hard work. That it involves perspiration, angst, and
self-sacrifice.

Doing art is as natural as falling asleep, as easy as brushing
your teeth.

Yes, it takes commitment. Yes, it takes time. But what, pray
tell, is wrong with that? Name one better use of time than ac-
cessing the portal to the imagination? Would you really rather be
figuring your taxes, shopping for things you don't need?

As my friend Bob Savino says in his wonderful book *As the
Spirit Moves*, "Why gnaw on the rind when you can savor the fruit?"

"But I'm not creative," you still insist on wailing.

Somewhere along the line we picked up the erroneous notion
that doing art was excruciating except for the few lucky souls who
are naturally "good at it."

95

Where did we get this erroneous notion? Certainly not from children. To a six-year-old, picking up a paintbrush, dipping it in a pot of paint, and rubbing it on a piece of paper is as natural as skipping or humming "Mary Had a Little Lamb." It's definitely a lot more natural than sitting still at dinner or tying a shoe.

What's hard is spending time doing meaningless things, following the cheap trinkets that may look good on the outside but are as hollow as a piñata on the inside. When you're in the arms of your imagination, you can dance unfettered on the moon.

"If you grew up in an African culture, you'd never think to question whether or not you were an artist," says David Darling, a former cellist with the Paul Winter Consort. "It's a simple extension of what we are as human beings."

That's why Darling, who has seven highly acclaimed recordings, an international concert schedule, and a prestigious movie soundtrack, started "Music for People" workshops that teach everyone to be a musician.

Teach is probably the wrong word because, as Darling says, "The concept that only certain people who play the right notes are musicians is unthinkable to someone in a tribal African culture. Music is simply joyful soundmaking, a celebration of movement and dance. It's part of a ritual honoring life."

Like so many things, we've cut off this part of ourselves that loves to sing. We were told by well-meaning teachers that our middle C was off key and that our exuberant meter didn't mesh with the quartet. Once again, we shut off part of the electricity.

At this point in your adult life, you'd probably rather French-kiss a copperhead than sing in public. The shower—well, maybe—but, as far as you're concerned, musical ability was like the fabled tortoise—it left you in the dust years ago.

Darling asks his students to hit themselves on the forehead every time they notice a negative thought coming up. Such niggling thoughts such as:

"I'm flubbing up."

"I can't sing."

"Sister Mary Margaret told me back in fourth grade I couldn't carry a tune in a bucket."

Before you know it, you look around the room and notice everyone is hitting himself in the forehead—even the professionals who also come to Darling's workshops. He has worked with everyone from Bobby ("Don't Worry Be Happy") McFerrin to Spyro Gyro and Peter, Paul and Mary.

"Feeling unworthy is so prevalent in the world that it's really amazing that human beings can feel good about anything," Darling says.

In his wildly provocative workshops, Darling offers a wide collection of unusual instruments, things you probably wouldn't find in your typical symphony orchestra. Darling's eclectic collection includes everything from accordions, banjos, and Japanese temple bells to kazoos, saws, and zithers.

After all, it's pretty hard to be too pretentious about music when you're playing a Mayan rain stick whose soft, lyrical rattle comes from the termite droppings inside.

This is what we need, to approach art in a less pretentious way. Let's get out the kazoos, the finger paints, the pots and pans that we used to bang on as kids.

"We've lost the sense of playing," Darling says. "We've disconnected from those dimensions of ourselves that our imaginations find so naturally."

Adults, instead of encouraging us to play, tell us to "go practice," he says.

From the time you were a kid, you were taught to check your imagination at the door. Your imaginary friend, the one who whispered secrets in your ear, the one who knows all about skipping and jumping rope, wasn't invited to school, to church, to the important "events" in life.

Invite her back. Send out a proper invitation. Draw it on the back of your grocery bag.

DESIGN THE COVER OF
YOUR AUTOBIOGRAPHY

It's Me!

Maybe you just want a full-size shot of your face with the title of
your book embedded in your front left tooth. Or maybe you'd rather
show your scrapbook from sixth grade or the first-place trophy you
won in that summer's gunnysack race.

What color will your book be? Will it have lots of words? A
fancy subtitle? Remember, you're the designer. What would best
represent you to the rest of the world?

More Fun Stuff

Create a character for *Saturday Night Live*.

Frame some leaves.

Make a Valentine's card for the "one that got away."

You're in Good Company

Erica Jong could only write *Fear of Flying* because she was sure it would never be published. When that proved to be wrong, Jong was so anxious about her family's reaction to her raunchy novel that she considered withdrawing it from publication.

INFAMOUS ANGELS

Before singer-songwriter Iris DeMent cut her first album, *Infamous Angels*, she worked at Kmart in Nashville, Tennessee.

Before she wrote her first song, she suffered from the same self-doubt and insecurity that all of us do. She'd write one line, tear it up, and convince herself it was useless because she'd never measure up to her heroes—Loretta Lynn, Merle Haggard, the Carter Family.

Even though she grew up in a family of musicians (not professional musicians, but church musicians who sang from their hearts, who sang from that God of their soul), she was just too intimidated to finish a song. One or two lines, sure. But never a whole song.

Finally, when she was twenty-five, she took a creative writing class. In that class she gained enough confidence to pursue her art—regardless of what anybody else thought.

EIGHTEEN

WEEK

"I made a conscious decision to stop running from things that I loved and just did it. Even if nobody liked it, even if it got me nowhere, even if everybody laughed, I was going to write songs and was going out to sing them," she says.

Needless to say, Kmart never got its clerk back. Iris DeMent has written three CDs (*Infamous Angel*, *My Life*, and *The World As It Should Be*), has been praised by critics of all genres, and has been asked to perform with nearly all the heroes she used to be intimidated by. Her song "Our Town" was chosen as the swan song for the last episode in the hit TV series *Northern Exposure*.

Hard to believe somebody that talented would ever suffer self-doubt.

I tell you this story about Iris because it opens our eyes to the humanness of our heroes. They're just as scared and as vulnerable as we are. Many of us make the mistake of assuming that the great masters get up each morning, pour a cup of coffee, and commence to pour out genius. We forget that all we're seeing is the end product.

Because they show us the stars and the moon and because they transport us to places we've never been before, we forget that somebody had to pack a suitcase.

Remember when Dorothy's dog, Toto, pulled back the curtain that hid "The Great and Terrible Oz"? After all that work getting the broom, all those encounters with flying monkeys, all that intimidation, Dorothy and her friends discover that the Great Oz is an everyday Joe just like them.

That's the best description I can come up with for this week's theme. We're going to knock down pedestals and come to realize that working artists are no different than you and me. They haven't conquered their shaking knees. They simply kept on working anyway.

Sir Laurence Olivier suffered tremendous stage fright, novelist E. B. White oftentimes felt like an impostor, and Hemingway was so sure he'd lost his gift that he took out a gun and shot himself.

101

It's important to know these things.

In fact, the only *real* difference between you and "them" is they keep on scribbling and shooting film even when their hearts are pounding and their flying monkeys are squawking.

They keep at it.

Often what we mistake as insecurity is simply lack of experience. We haven't practiced our breaststrokes long enough to learn to swim.

By the time Michelangelo landed a commission to paint the Sistine Chapel, he had done hundreds of thousands of simple sketches. His first sketches probably weren't that different than yours or mine. In fact, this is what he said: "If people knew how hard I worked, it wouldn't seem so wonderful at all."

It's quantity that begets quality.

Genius can only step in after we've practiced, after we've relaxed enough to step aside, to surrender to our own souls and let the God of our being slide on through.

But the first step will always be acknowledging that it's possible. Realizing that you're no different than the artists you admire. Realizing that you can do the same things they do. Realizing that their struggles and victories are the same ones that haunt you.

So it's really your call. You can put in the hours or not. But whatever you do, don't lose sight of the fact that behind the curtain of William Faulkner, Georgia O'Keeffe, and Marcel Duchamp is a guy who catches the flu and gets pimples just like you.

INVENT SOMETHING TO MAKE
YOUR WORLD BETTER

Edison or Bust

There's some pet peeve that's been bugging you since you were twelve years old—the paper carrier who throws the paper in the bushes or coffee that doesn't stay warm very long. C'mon, something is bubbling up inside your brain about now.

You don't have to actually make the device that will solve the problem—although you might want to—but do come up with some solution to this nagging problem. For example, if you want your coffee to stay warm longer, maybe you could design an insulated mug or a heater to plug it in to.

One woman hated the way her pet always bounced around when she took him to the vet. She invented doggie seat belts that, at last report, were selling like hotcakes. *People* magazine even wrote a story about her.

Make a sock monkey or some other
stuffed animal.

Buy a gift for less than five dollars
and wrap it creatively. Don't forget to
give it away.

Draw a picture of your first-grade
classroom.

You're in Good Company

Julia Roberts says she often "fakes it" when she
doesn't know how to do something.

Week 19

There is only one real deprivation . . . and that is not to be able
to give one's gifts to those one loves most.

MAY SARTON

TEA FOR TWO

Even though God is always with us, always helping us create,
sometimes we need someone more human to remind us. That's
why it's vital to find an art partner, someone you can talk to about
your artistic goals, fears, and accomplishments.

This week, you're going to find that special soulmate. You're
going to seek out someone with whom you can meet on a weekly
basis. It doesn't have to be a four-hour commitment. Maybe you'll
want to do it over the phone. But you must enlist someone who is
willing to pay witness to your art every single week. You're looking for someone who is willing to hear what you have to say, who
is genuinely interested in the thoughts and feelings sashaying
through your soul.

It's a little like cheerleader tryouts. The person who wins this
coveted position (and this is a highly sought-after position) is
going to be "rah-rah-rahing" you every week. He's going to be-

lieve in you, encourage you, pat you on the back for faithfully showing up and doing your art.

Notice I didn't say a critic, but a cheerleader. This is an important distinction. The last thing you need right now is someone who's going to put her finger down her throat when she hears your poem about the neighbor's puppy or someone who tries to convince you that the right-hand corner of your painting needs a little more fuchsia.

No way! That person needs a long vacation to Siberia. By herself.

If you feel a little funny about asking someone for this much time, remember that you are offering a gift. Not only will you be doing the same thing for him (listening, seeing, and rah-rahing), but you are offering the gift of who you are.

This person gets the privilege of really getting to know you. Not the you that got the shoplifting conviction in junior high or the you that flunked out of sixth grade. Those are petty things that you did as a human.

No, this person is getting a ringside seat to the you that is really you. The God you, the richer, deeper you that you might now have had the privilege of getting to know yourself. And that, my friend, is a rare and priceless gift. Witnessing the authentic, God-like side of a person always raises the person who witnesses it to a higher level.

Oftentimes we show up to our friends and family as our little selves, the selves that obsess, the selves that eat too much sugar. It's no wonder we have problems getting along. But the *big* you, the artist you that is willing to stand naked and unafraid, gives nothing but gifts. Trust me! You will inspire your partner. And she will be glad you asked. She will be grateful that she knows you as she does.

Maybe you already know someone who is willing to play this part in your budding new artistic career. If not, post a sign at the local theater or library or hobby shop. Run a personals ad. Someone is out there.

Audacious, but reverent artist seeks audacious, but reverent partner.

Call _____
(this is where you put your name)

at: _____
(this is where you put your phone number)

It's probably better to choose someone you're not already in a rut with—like your husband or your best friend. No offense, but familiar relationships tempt us to stay in our ruts. These get-togethers are meant to be fresh, raw, and alive.

I could give you a lot of rules on how to do it, but I trust that like the process of art opens you to a deeper knowing, this process of meeting and sharing with your partner will happen naturally too.

I *will* suggest that you make two commitments. First, you meet every week. You're in charge of working out the details. At first, it may seem like a pain—finding time to meet every week, carving out the space in your already bulging day-timer. But eventually there will be nothing more important. It's a little like the launching of a project. At first, you're not sure you *really* want to, but once you get going, it's a greased slide down easy street.

Rule number two: Never judge or critique each other's work. Yes, you show each other your work—proudly, boldly—but never make comments or suggestions. You are here to encourage. Your job is to say "yeah" and give brownie points for the fact that your partner showed up and did the work. Period. That is all that is important. Showing up. Doing the work. God is taking care of the rest.

Why does having an art partner work? Some of us, unfortunately, have this slight flaw regarding commitments to ourselves. Who are we anyway but the slimy slugs on the totem pole of life? But if we know someone else (someone important?) is counting on us to read a poem or perform a skit, we'll somehow find the time to do it.

I'll close this week with a true story I heard about a Sunday school teacher in Kentucky. One Sunday, a new little boy named Tommy comes bounding into her classroom. Tommy is bright, vivacious, and happy, but he was born without a left arm. The teacher welcomes him, silently wishing she'd known he was coming so she could have explained to the other children about the importance of being understanding toward those who are different. But before she can give it much thought, one of the boys is pulling hair, another is tearing leaves off a plant. To keep peace, she starts in on a familiar fingerplay.

"Here is the church. . . . Here are the people."

She stops suddenly, aghast that she could have been so insensitive. She looks over at Tommy, whose right hand, joined with the left hand of one of the girls in the class, is joyfully making a steeple.

Together, we can build almost anything—a steeple, a play, a new way of being.

You and Me Against the World

Here's an example of what you and your compatriot might share.

First, we'll share our artistic goals.

Since I'm the one who made this up, I'll go first.

My all-encompassing goal is to open to spirit, to get my ego—or, as Emerson said, "my bloated little nothingness"—out of the way. I want my art to speak for God, for wholeness, for healing. Right now, I'm still scared a lot of the time. I'm intimidated by writers who look so much better than me, who say profound things, who are funnier than me. But I know I must make myself vulnerable, be willing to be small and to say what's mine to say.

Okay, your turn.

_____

_____

_____

_____

_____

(continued on next page)

(continued from previous page)

_____

_____

_____

_____

_____

_____

Hey, that's pretty cool. I knew I picked a great art partner. Now, I'll tell you about the projects I'm working on. Not all of them are "in motion"—at least not in my computer. But if they've crossed my mind at all, if I've thought of them at some time or another, they are truly "in motion" somewhere. They're trying to break through. Here goes:

1. I've written a rough draft (*rough* being the operative word here) of a screenplay about four unwed moms who find their inner strength. The script revolves around these characters:

    *   Tinker—a loose, gum-chomping high school dropout who has no idea who the father of her baby is.

    *   Jai—a fifteen-year-old gang member whose boyfriend gets shot by an opposing gang before she even breaks the news about the baby.

    *   Deena—a rich, perky, blond cheerleader who played Aunt Eller in the school musical. Her parents kick her out of the house when she refuses to have an abortion.

- McQueen—a hard-working black girl who finds her boyfriend in the dressing room of the store they own together with a homely white chick.

All four of them find themselves at a Christian home for unwed moms. Their nemesis is Clara Applebaum, the rigid, uptight director of the home.

2. I'm also working on a children's book called *The Trouble with Grown-ups*. Not that I can take credit for it. It woke me up one night and I merely took notes. I'm thinking about illustrating it myself.

3. My daughter's favorite line is "Mom, tell me about when you were a kid! Puh-lease." I've told her all the stories I can remember so I promised to write her a book of my memoirs. I know when I sit down to write it, I'll remember more. The commitment, as I said, opens the door.

4. I'd like to put a team together to produce *Jung and the Wristless*, a live soap opera I developed with six characters who show up every week at a twelve-step meeting. Even though my acting experience stops at charades, I'd like to play one of the characters.

5. I'd like to syndicate my travel column, "Now, Where Was I?"

6. I'd also like to syndicate this series I work on from time to time with "little known facts" about celebrities. Did you know, for example, that Tom Cruise once considered becoming a priest?

Okay, those are my big dreams and creative projects for the moment. *(continued on next page)*

(continued from previous page)

Now it's your turn.

_____

_____

_____

_____

_____

_____

_____

_____

_____

_____

_____

_____

_____

_____

_____

_____

_____

FIND YOUR OWN SPECIAL PLACE

Honey, I'm Home

In the book *The Education of Little Tree*, a story about a Native American boy raised by his grandparents, Little Tree is advised to find his own special place. His grandmother tells him, "This is where you go to feel alive, where you feel the closest to God." Your place might be a park or a mountain near your home. It might be a coffeehouse where you can sketch the sexy waiter or other customers. It might be an overstuffed chair in your den where you wrap yourself in a favorite afghan. The only criterion is it be a place that you feel is all yours, where you can find the peace and quiet to enjoy your own company.

Clip coupons for things you don't
want and leave them on shelves near
the products.

Photocopy your face.

Study a saint.

You're in Good Company

Vincent van Gogh once worried that he didn't have
what he needed to be creative. He felt like a man
"whose heart is imprisoned."

WEEK
twenty

TO MOON OR NOT TO MOON

To Patch Adams, that is the question. Not that the rebellious doctor immortalized in the 1998 movie starring Robin Williams has to think about it very long. He has been known to bare his behind at professional meetings, association banquets, graduation ceremonies, and other oh-so-serious events. He's currently planning a big fund-raiser in Phoenix called Full Moon Over Camelback, where thousands of people pay twenty-five dollars for the privilege of mooning the city in unison at the stroke of midnight.

As charity events go, it's pure genius—no overhead, no auctions, no selling things nobody really wants anyway.

Patch, who says he can't conceive of practicing medicine without creativity, insists art is every bit as essential to diagnosis and treatment as the surgical suite or the hydrotherapy room. Without art, he says, life is sterile and meaningless.

Patch, of course, has turned his whole life into a piece of art. *Normal* is a word he can barely pronounce, let alone live up to. He speaks his mind and doesn't care who agrees.

Anything, as far as he's concerned, is possible.

If you saw the movie, you already know he's building the world's first "silly hospital," where doctors wear clown noses, patients eat dinner with their caregivers, and everybody performs skits, draws cartoons, and clowns around. All services are free.

Eventually, he wants the world to own a big jet so when disasters happen (like in Kosovo or Littleton), clowns and musicians can fly in to spread love.

And why not? What we're doing now certainly isn't working.

Patch says the majority of adults in this country are bored, lonely, and afraid. In fact, Patch believes the world's biggest problem is that none of us know how to have fun anymore.

He claims we're all wallowing in misery and that one of the most radical things a person can do is have a good day.

In fact, he claims the best way to serve mankind is to figure out a way to enjoy yourself (yes, it's something you have to *decide* to do) and to let people know that enjoying yourself is a good thing. As simple as that sounds, most people think having fun is a waste of time or, more accurately, something they have no control over.

Patch says it's an intentional decision. He *decided* to live this way. He has made himself into who he is—who he wanted to be. He is never sick, never has a bad day. He is constantly and consistently outrageous.

Most days, for example, he wears a clown suit. Of course, he also owns a gorilla costume. And a ballet tutu. And for someone who is six foot six with hair down to his waist, that's not a look likely to show up on the cover of *Vanity Fair*. He gives himself exercises to do—like call fifty names in the phone book to practice making conversation. Once, he went into a bar and refused to leave until he'd heard every patron's story.

We must decide to be audacious. Patch suggests injecting surprise, fun, and outrageousness into each day. Great freedom comes in taking risks, stepping over that tiny little line that society prescribes as "normal."

Patch reminds us that we often live in other people's ruts, that we do most things without thinking about them. Because we think we have to. Or because we're conditioned that way. It doesn't even cross our minds that we could try something else.

We don't spend enough time in the absurd zone, where the world looks crazy. Patch, by the way, doesn't care if anybody laughs when he clowns around. He's not doing it for you. It's for him. And this is an important point. You have to cultivate a little bit of that don't-give-a-shit attitude.

Even those of us who pretend not to give a shit actually do. We worry if the kids have the right tennis shoes, whether the weather stripping is going to last.

Patch says this "worry" is what causes most medical problems, this desire to follow the rules and "be normal."

He suggests making an ass out of yourself every day—until it no longer feels uncomfortable. You can start with what Patch calls "ridiculous raiment," clothes that clash and are loud and bright. Given the narrowness of fashion standards, it's not too difficult to come up with something that will make people chuckle, point, and realize that maybe there are "other possibilities." Patch recommends fire hats, space helmets, and beanies with whirring propellers.

Okay, so maybe you're not ready to overhaul your wardrobe, but the question you must ask yourself is, "What can I do to have a good day? How can I have a little fun?"

Not just today. But every day.

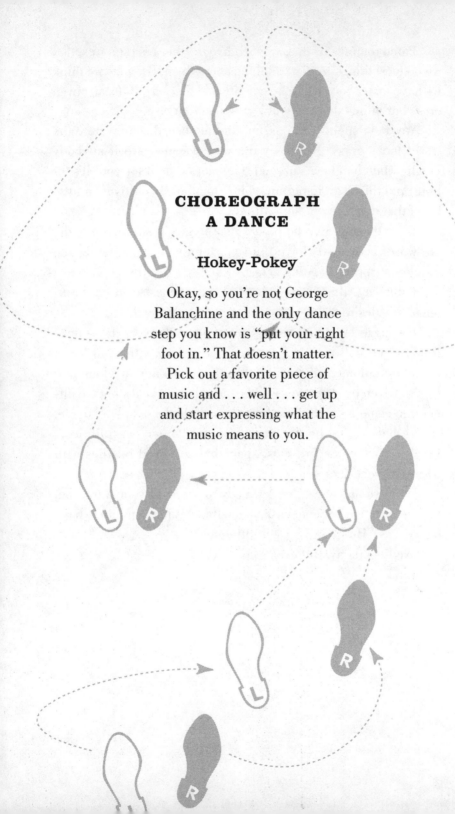

CHOREOGRAPH
A DANCE

Hokey-Pokey

Okay, so you're not George
Balanchine and the only dance
step you know is "put your right
foot in." That doesn't matter.
Pick out a favorite piece of
music and . . . well . . . get up
and start expressing what the
music means to you.

More Fun Stuff

Stage a Monopoly tournament.

Anonymously send your favorite poem to twenty people.

Dress in a sexy costume (or something unlike you) and go out for a night on the town.

You're in Good Company

Composer Lukas Foss says, "I've been composing since age seven and I still do not know where notes will come from when I accept a commission for a new work."

> What are the best things and worst things
> in your life and when are you going to
> get around to whispering them or shouting them?
>
> **RAY BRADBURY**

FINDING TIME

Say it one last time if you must, but after this week, you will never again need to utter the world's most famous excuse:

> "I really *want* to, but I can't find
> the time."

I'm not denying that most of us are overcommitted, overstretched, overburdened.

But I do have to ask this question: Why?

Do you really need to have your nails done every week? Do you really need to gossip with your sister for an hour every night? Are those reruns of *Roseanne* really that important to your well-being?

Yep, this week, we're going to learn how to scrape out the time to write your novel, practice your guitar, take those long-lusted-after acting lessons.

Don't expect me to suggest something unoriginal like "get up thirty minutes earlier" or "devote the last fifteen minutes of your lunch hour to developing plot points." That type of ho-hum strategy you can figure out on your own. Heck, you probably tried the get-up-thirty-minutes-early strategy last New Year's when you resolved to aerobicize to Kathy Smith every morning.

No, my first tip is stay in bed thirty minutes *longer*. Spend that time dreaming. Fill yourself up with magic. When mystery and passion fill your soul, finding time is easier than getting into Bill Clinton's pants.

Gandhi used to say that if he had a busy day, he simply had to add meditation to his "to do" list. Otherwise, he'd never get everything done.

Strategy two: Make the novel, the screenplay, whatever it is you want to work on "no big deal." The real reason most of us can't find time is our annoying tendency toward perfectionism. If the novel doesn't have to read like James Joyce, we could probably sneak in a sentence or two between appointments, while the kids are playing hide-and-seek in the basement.

So instead of waiting for time, grab time; steal it like an ornery eight-year-old who shoves a cookie in his pocket the minute Mom looks the other way. Steal it while you're waiting for the train, on your coffee break, while your husband is plucking his nose hairs.

The old "I'll do it when I have time" is a fairy tale, like Santa Claus and the tooth fairy. Wake up, Virginia. Huge lump sums of time do not exist.

Lawyer Scott Turow was able to write all 431 pages of *Presumed Innocent* on the Chicago commuter train.

Strategy three: Give up self-sabotage. I find that if I give up self-loathing (this is a sport I've won several gold medals in), I have all kinds of free time. It takes gallons of energy to continually tell myself what a excrementitious piece of monkey vomit I am. Each of us gets only so many units of energy. If we use up 35 or more of our allotted 100 units on low-flying shame, guilt, and the realization that yesterday's four pages needs to be carved into thousands of tiny pieces and shoved down the garbage disposal, we only have 65 of our valuable energy units left.

And while we're on the subject, let's move on to number four, which is to give up every single thing that isn't enriching your life. C'mon, admit it. You spend a lot of time doing things that you'd rather not be doing, things that you do only because you've always done them. Or because somebody told you that was how they were done.

As Toni Morrison once said, "We are traditionally rather proud of ourselves for having slipped creative work in there between the domestic chores and obligations. I'm not sure we deserve such big A-pluses for that."

I urge you to start living intentionally, to really ask yourself, "Is how I spend my time bringing me joy? Is it making my life bigger? If not, why in the heck am I still doing it?"

Yeah, maybe my daughter can't find her soccer uniform and the litter box needs to be changed and there's a sale on cat food at the Piggly Wiggly and I need to call my friend Ivy in Tucson and buy a birthday card for Bob's forty-ninth birthday and there's a war in Kosovo and the threat of global warming and I need to quit eating so many Krispy Kremes, start drinking more water, remember to wear sunscreen. And did I mention the *Star Trek* video is overdue?

But I'm going to get out my screenplay and write just one sentence anyway.

WRITE YOUR
MISSION STATEMENT

Mission Possible

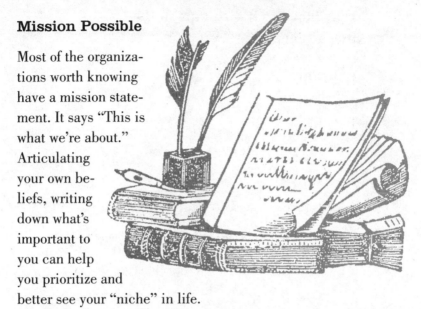

Most of the organizations worth knowing have a mission statement. It says "This is what we're about." Articulating your own beliefs, writing down what's important to you can help you prioritize and better see your "niche" in life.

SARK, the artist/author who first roared into public consciousness with her *How to Be an Artist* poster, says her life's mission is "to free creative spirits everywhere." To do this, she wears pajamas to work, takes naps, and draws on the walls.

Play hopscotch with tape in the
living room.

Dress like a nun.

Kiss five people.

You're in Good Company

Madeleine L'Engle's *A Wrinkle in Time* was rejected
by dozens of publishers.

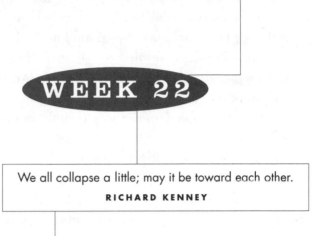

WEEK 22

We all collapse a little; may it be toward each other.
RICHARD KENNEY

PUT IT IN A SONG

I just woke up and read about the high school massacre in Littleton, Colorado. Twelve man-cubs killed in cold blood. Killed by other man-cubs—babies, really—who couldn't conjure even a shred of hope, their minds warped and then blinded by anger. It's all I can do to steady myself here in my chair. I want to run to the bathroom and vomit, to beat my fists against something hard and unyielding.

How could my country, the one I pledged allegiance to every morning for six years of grade school, have come to this?

Even though there is life to be lived today, a daughter to take to preschool (surely, these "schools" for four- and five-year-olds will be spared), a project to collate, this book to write, I feel drawn to this tragedy. I'm tempted to sit comatose by the television set, to watch the horror and shake my head.

I'm sure CNN, if not dispensing play-by-play commentary, is at least giving updates—facts about the killers, maudlin stories about the victims, tear-drenched stories from people who survived.

Yet, the mourning dove still sits on her eggs in a flower pot on my front porch. She sits there trembling as loud humans barge in and out the door that's only feet from her offspring. She sits there even though last year, a horrible storm knocked over the flower pot, sending her eggs crashing to the concrete below. She sits there even though death is imminent and life is cruel.

A part of me wants to hide, to take Tasman and flee to New Zealand, where her dad owns a winery and, presumably, a more peaceful existence.

But it's not a time to run away or to sit numb, helplessly devouring all the details.

It's a time to act, a time to create. A time for making peace out of chaos, a time for spinning love out of the threads of incomprehension.

It's easy for me to think, "How can I, one insignificant person from Kansas, stop a groundswell?"

But that's me forgetting who I am.

I am a creator, made in the image and likeness of the Great Creator. My ideas come straight from the mind of God.

And I am not insignificant.

If nothing else, I can write about what the massacre means to me. I know nothing about it, really. The names haven't even been released. The macabre details are still being gathered. Other than a loquacious dentist from Littleton who happened to be cross-country skiing at the same resort as I last winter, I have no real ties to this suburb of Denver.

Yet the story is also about me. It's about my anger, the many times I wanted revenge when someone rejected me. It's about the times I lashed out when someone said "good-bye" or "You're not what I'm looking for" or "You're too needy, too depressed, too tall."

It's about the unhealed places in all of our hearts, those wounds that make us want to hit someone back.

Why do we want to hit someone back? Because we feel pow-

126

erless. Because we have forgotten who we are. We have forgotten that the life force of the Creator thrums through our very veins.

It's easy to forget in this culture of convenience. No longer do we make our own bread, sing our own songs, dance our own jigs. No longer do we create much of anything. Too often we even forget that we can. The very thing that joins us to our Creator lies dormant.

And in this forgetting, we lose our footing. Picasso said that when he realized painting was a way to give form to his terrors and his desires, he knew he had found his way.

The boys who killed in Littleton had not yet found their way. They conned themselves into believing they were insignificant. They didn't know that the life force of the entire universe pulsed through their bodies. They hadn't yet come to appreciate the sacredness of each moment.

They didn't know they could have screamed their rage and rejection into a song. They didn't know they could have danced their anger into a profound acceptance of themselves and their pain.

If only they had known.

It's too late for them. But it's not too late for us, all of us just as guilty of anger and rage as the killers we point fingers at.

You are powerful. You can create the answers to the horrors that confront our country, the things that make us want to throw up our hands, flee to foreign countries, to kill.

Inside you is a stage play that will inspire someone to forgive instead of kill. Inside you is a painting or a story that will turn fear into hope, horror into peace. Even if it's peace in one person's heart, it is enough.

As Henry Miller once asked, "Where in this broad land is the holy of holies hidden?"

It's in the mourning dove still sitting on her eggs. It's in you.

PLANT YOUR FAMILY TREE

Oaks, Elms, and Joneses

What do you know about the country from which your family hails? How did they get from there to here? Do you know the story of your ancestors? If possible, plan a trip to your heritage homeland. Perhaps you still have distant cousins there.

Think of Alex Haley. He became a household name when he sat down and dug up his family tree. Your roots are just as interesting. *How to Trace Your Family Tree* by the American Genealogy Research Institute might help.

More Fun Stuff

Do a rain dance.

Make something ethnic.

Stage a poetry reading around a campfire.

You're in Good Company

At the writing program at Stanford, classmates Thomas McGuane, Larry McMurtry, and Ken Kesey were not even remotely the best writers.

WEEK Twenty-three

We must accept that
this creative pulse within us is
God's creative pulse itself.

JOSEPH CHILTON PEARCE

THE *G* WORD

This is the week that may be hardest to swallow. The week where
we consider the radical notion that God *wants* to help you with
your creative projects, that He actually supports the idea of your
becoming an artist.

I know what most of you think. That God lives millions of
miles away, that He's so busy working on world hunger that He
has no time left over to help you throw a pot or design a center-
piece. You can buy that He "moves mountains," but you can't
fathom that He might also have some good thoughts for scene
three in your screenplay.

Either that or we want to steer as far away from God as possible. After all, who wants to paint crucifixes or sketch portraits
of the Last Supper? Drive those irrational thoughts from your
head. God is all about expanding, not about being stuck in little

boxes with crosses, halos, and the Ten Commandments. God shows up in many forms.

Early on, we put limits on God. We start to see Him as somebody like . . . oh, say . . . us.

Instead of believing we were made in His image and likeness, we started making Him in our own. As Anne Lamott once said, you can safely assume you've created God in your own image when it turns out that God hates all the same people you do.

So our first step is to get over the God that we made up. The God that's stingy and angry and wears a Led Zeppelin beard. We've got to consider the possibility that He might actually like us, that He's somebody who supports us in our wildest dreams, somebody like Santa Claus or June Cleaver.

We've got to believe that He'll be there for us and that if we ask for help with our projects, He'll send a thousand unseen helping hands, as Joseph Campbell so aptly put it.

We've got to get over this idea that following our dreams is not God's will for us. Just who do you think it was that planted that dream in your heart anyway? Where do you think that big idea came from? Our creative dreams come straight from God.

God has lots of ideas for novels and sculptures and photographs.

God, in case you forgot, is the Great Creator. He was the first artist, the big cheese from which all the rest of us come. And as Julia Cameron points out, artists have a thing for other artists.

Why wouldn't God want you to create? Why wouldn't He want you to follow in His footsteps? He gave you the ability to dream and to create. Does He also have to give you the paintbrush?

Somewhere along the line, we picked up the preposterous notion that God's will for us has something to do with starving children in Africa. We believe that *our* wills for our lives are in direction opposition to God's will. We figure He wants us to wear ashes on our heads, to bow and to keep repeating, "Forgive me, Father, for I have sinned."

131

Nothing could be further from the truth. God's will for you is complete and total happiness, and if painting or writing will make you happy, then God is all for it.

If you take a step in the direction of your dreams, He'll be right behind you with a host of heavenly cheerleaders, giving you the high five and saying, "You go, girl."

This cheerleading squad, by the way, is equally available to everyone. God does not play favorites.

God is not practical. He's not stingy. He's not any of the things that you and I are. He'll be as generous as you will let Him.

Probably the person in my lifetime who had the most direct line to God was Mother Teresa. And although she did take a vow of poverty, she knew good and well that her God was big and abundant and capable of anything.

Once when she needed funds for a project in India, she wrote to this prestigious American corporation and asked for a half million dollars. The corporation agreed that her request was a worthy one. They called her in and proudly presented her with a check for $250,000.

She said, "But I asked for a half million."

The board president explained that they had considered her request and that this was all they could do.

She bowed her head and said, "Then we need to pray."

They prayed and, sure enough, the board of directors retreated to a private meeting room and came back a few minutes later with another check, this time for $100,000.

Once again, Mother Teresa said, "We need to pray."

Guess who got $500,000?

Most of us would have accepted the $250,000. But Mother Teresa knew. She knew God wasn't limited.

Our God is big. And He has big plans.

As Mother Teresa said, "We need to pray."

BECOME AN EXPERT AT SOMETHING

Ph.D.

Think of some subject you're interested in and then learn everything you can about it. Maybe it's Tasmanian devils. Or making
art from recycled egg cartons. Or growing herbs or programming
computers. It doesn't matter how large or small the topic—it's just
important to be passionate about something. Are there others out
there interested in this subject too? Maybe you can join a club—
or start one.

More Fun Stuff

Make a whole chorus of snow angels.
(If it's now summer, maybe it's time to
catch that jar of fireflies.)

Eat four new fruits.

Learn to yodel. Do it in a public place.

You're in Good Company

Raymond Chandler was well past forty by the time
he started writing.

WEEK 24

It took fifteen years to discover I had no talent for writing, but I couldn't
give it up because, by then, I was too famous.

ROBERT BENCHLEY

GOD AS CEO

Twelve years ago, when I launched my freelance writing career, I
appointed God as my CEO.

Although, in looking back, I realize it was probably Him who
hired me.

At the time, I was trying to decide whether or not to write full-
time. I was working twenty hours a week for a small company and
writing on the side.

"God," I prayed, "I really like Resource and Development
[the place I was working], but I have this dream, you see, of being
a full-time freelancer. It's not that I don't like writing fund-raising
letters, it's just that I want to pursue my own story ideas, write
about the things that burn in my heart. What do You think?"

Already, I was getting lots of assignments. Big national magazines were calling. I was making new contacts, receiving nibbles

on a couple of column ideas. That would have been answer enough for some people.

But I'm dense. I wanted an unquestionable sign.

The next day I got fired.

Another time, when my freelancing was slow, I sent out résumés, something I'm prone to do whenever I feel panicky. Sure enough, I was offered a job within a few weeks. The offer, writing marketing materials for a local busline (okay, I didn't say I was offered an interesting job), was for more money than I'd ever made in my life. But how could I afford to give up all that time?

Was I really ready to give up my freelancing career? I figured I'd better consult God. Again, I prayed for a clear sign. But this time I upped the stakes. I told Him He'd better speak up within twenty-four hours because that's when I needed to give my employer-to-be a yea or a nay.

The very next morning, *Travel & Leisure*, the magazine I most wanted to write for, called to give me an assignment.

After I hung up, yelled "Yes!" and did the goal line hootchie-koo, I bowed my head and said, "Thanks." But God must have been in the mood to show off that day, because not fifteen minutes later, another magazine that I'd never even heard of, let alone sent a query to, called and wanted a story about steaks. My hometown is famous for barbecue, steaks, and other vein-clogging cuisine.

I had to call and tell my boss-to-be "Thanks, but no thanks."

So does God answer our creative prayers? Ask Him tonight and find out.

CREATE A FAMILY CREST

But Do You Get Fewer Cavities?

Back in their ancestral country, most families had a crest or a coat of arms. It often depicted the family's line of work or special attributes (such as courage or valor or whatever made them stand out). You can design your own crest. Don't try dodging this with some excuse like "I can't draw." Keep the spirit of the exercise in mind and keep it simple. Make a mosaic if you need to.

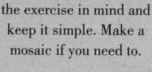

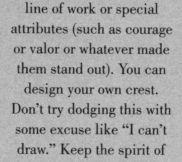

   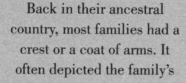

Plant a plant you've never heard of.

Create a new daytime game show.

Make a crossword puzzle.

You're in Good Company

Richard Hooker worked for seven years on his humorous war novel, *MASH*, only to have it rejected by twenty-one publishers before Morrow decided to publish it. It became a runaway best-seller and spawned a blockbuster movie and a highly successful TV series.

139

WeeK 25

Adventures don't begin until you get into the forest.
That first step is an act of faith.

MICKEY HART, GRATEFUL DEAD DRUMMER

D.I.A.

I might as well get it out now. I sometimes suffer from depression. I don't really like to admit it. I think it makes me sound weak. Inferior. At least a notch or two below Kim Basinger.

When the big D tightens its ugly claws around me, I put on the boxing gloves and wage war. Unfortunately, it's always against myself.

"Well, Pam," is how it usually starts. "If you were really this vibrant, together person you claim to be, you could kickbox this thing out the door. Where's your willpower, anyway?"

And then it goes downhill. "Who would ever want you? You're a disgrace, no good to anyone."

And then I get really mean.

A friend (perhaps I should say a *former* friend) once told me that we humans are meant to live our lives from "glory to glory." My life pretty much moves from glory to darkness to glory again, which isn't too bad except when you're in the dark parts.

140

It doesn't make it any easier knowing it runs in my family. My maternal grandmother had "nervous breakdowns," when she'd disappear for a few weeks and come back with no explanation to anyone. My brother has been hospitalized a couple times for what we can at least now name as clinical depression.

One therapist I consulted wrote my problem off with this comment: "Ah, you're a writer, a creative person [said as if it was a malady comparable to having an extra arm or a blinking antenna growing out of my head]. Creative people just have these problems. There's really nothing you can do."

And for this I paid sixty dollars?

Luckily, I found out that there is something I can do. And it's only by complete accident that I found out. It was ten o'clock, the night before a creativity class I was facilitating. I was really feeling depressed. The class assignment—making a sculpture of some kind—was about as appealing as a blind date with Ted Bundy. All I wanted to do was get in bed and pull the covers over my head.

But I was the teacher. How could I rightly expect the other participants to bring in a sculpture if I didn't do it? I wrestled with it for a while. I even started composing excuses for why I didn't get the project done. My daughter had a bead up her nose. My computer had developed a brain tumor. I couldn't drive because my garage-door opener was broken.

There was this other voice, however, a beensy voice—as my daughter likes to call tiny things—that kept trying to get through. It whispered something about D.I.A.

"What?" I asked suspiciously. "D.I.A.? What in the heck is that?"

"Do it anyway!" the voice insisted.

Although I normally don't when I'm feeling like Sylvia Plath, I listened to this beensy voice. I decided to go ahead and attempt to tackle the project.

Somewhat reluctantly, I chose a picture I really liked of a girl jumping into the air for joy. She had on a peasant dress, her legs

141

were bent, her arms spread wide, and her head was held high in ecstasy. In other words, she looked exactly the opposite of how I felt.

I copied this picture at several different sizes—50 percent, 100 percent, 200 percent. I cut the copies out, mounted them on cardboard, added a Popsicle stick, and then made them stand, smallest to largest, on a cardboard tube. When I shone a light on the procession of happy, jumping girls, the largest one in the back made a shadow even larger on the wall behind it.

At about midnight, as I was packing up the light to take to class the next day, it suddenly occurred to me that my depression had lifted. No, that is an understatement. I actually felt happy, enlivened—kinda like the girl in the picture.

What a revelation. For once, I didn't listen to the voice that told me I was much too tired and depressed to make a stupid sculpture, the voice that insisted that the only rational thing to do was get in bed.

When you think about it, a voice that tells you you're as worthless as dog doo-doo is not a voice you really want to listen to.

The other voice, the one that can never be extinguished, thank God, is probably the one with my best interest at heart. And it told me to D.I.A.

I've had this lesson banged into my head time and time again. I don't feel like writing a chapter or I don't want to go to a class I signed up for. But then, if and when I do it anyway, I always feel better, I feel lifted up.

For years, I kept this unique sculpture in my bedroom, not only because I liked the sheer bliss this girl represented to me, but because it was a reminder that I *could* break out of the grips of inertia, that hovering cloud of depression. I did have a choice.

Not willpower, mind you: but choice.

It's always pretty simple. Which voice are you going to listen to? The voice that says, "You? An artist? You flunked Miss Brightly's art class. You have as much talent as a tsetse fly"?

Or the voice that says, "D.I.A."?

It has become my motto. And it was as simple as a pair of scissors and a cardboard tube.

D.I.A.

An important slogan to live by.

WRITE A MEMOIR OF YOUR FIRST DATE

The Dating Game

Don't tell me you can't remember your first date. Nothing inspires more emotions than outings with the opposite sex. What did you wear? Where did you go? What was your biggest fear? Did you ever go out with him or her again?

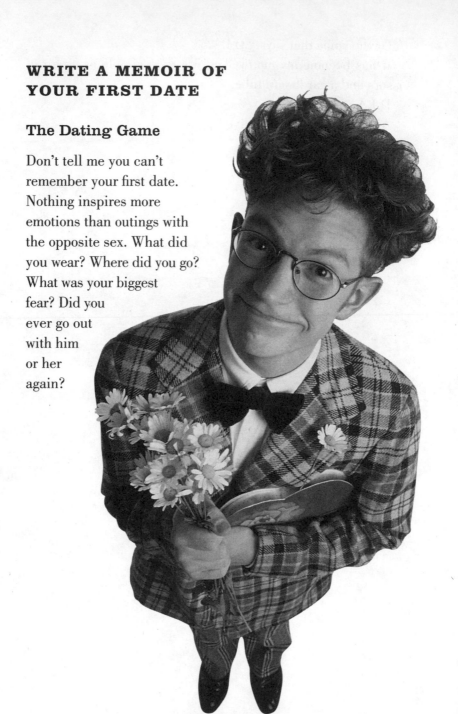

More Fun Stuff

Dress like your favorite movie character.

Audit a class.

Write a thank-you letter to God. Mail it.

You're in Good Company

Amy Tan set aside two half-completed manuscripts after she discussed the books so exhaustively that she lost her will to write them.

ONCE UPON A TIME

Every night, I read my daughter a story before she goes to bed. I started this sacred ritual while she was still in the womb, balancing such classics as *The Secret Garden* and *The Prince and the Pauper* on my growing belly.

When she was three, she started asking for stories that weren't in books, stories about when she was a baby, tales from my childhood, sagas from her heritage.

"Tell me the one with the pages inside you," she said one night.

She wanted to understand where she came from, how she fit in the whole big picture. She wanted me to tell her a story from my heart. I cleared my throat and began.

The Kalahari Bushmen believe that a man's story is his most sacred possession. They know something that we've forgotten in this country. Without a story, you haven't got a country or a culture or a civilization.

Week Twenty-six

One of actor James Woods' prized possessions is the canvas bag he used to deliver newspapers when he was a boy. A few years ago, his mother returned it to him with a note pinned to it. The note said, "Never forget where you came from. It will hold you in good stead."

Voices in the Night, Spinning Tales

★ Perhaps fiction's best storyteller was Scheherazade, whose life was spared for 1,001 Arabian nights because an enthralled sultan wanted to hear the end of her irresistible tales. In response to his first wife's betrayal, this rather heartless sultan vowed revenge against all women. He'd marry a different woman each night and then behead her first thing the next morning.

Scheherazade's tales of Aladdin, Ali Baba and the Forty Thieves, and Sinbad the Sailor so enticed the sultan that they cured his nasty case of misogyny. Not only did he spare Scheherazade's life, but he fell in love with her and liberated women everywhere.

★ Ivan the Terrible, who enjoyed the full privilege of being a tyrant, kept his own *Late, Late Show*—three storytellers who were always on hand to while away his insomnia. Today, of course, Ivan would be clicking his way through 198 cable channels.

★ Not a word of *The Iliad* or *The Odyssey* was written down, even though Homer is credited as "author." Rather he recited the epic poems from memory to his contemporaries in preliterate Greece, 1000 B.C.

Knowing and telling where you came from will indeed keep you in good stead.

When we fail to tell our story, we lose a part of ourselves. When we keep quiet, don't tell, we lose our footing.

147

Stories, if nothing else, liberate us. When we're able to tell our story we feel alive. That's why new love often feels so glorious. We've got an audience for our story, a brand-new person who hasn't yet heard about our joys and our sorrows. It's not that we're so smitten with this other person. We're smitten with ourselves, with the unique person that our stories are about. When love goes stale, it's often because we've quit telling stories.

Stories connect us to ourselves and to each other. Alice Walker once said that a story is different than advice because a story becomes part of the fabric of your whole soul, and has the ability to heal you.

In 400 B.C., Socrates was upset by the new fad—writing—because it threatened the storyteller's tradition. He declared: "The discovery of the alphabet will create forgetfulness in the learner's souls because they will not use their memories."

It's probably a good thing he never heard about satellite dishes and VCRs.

When we're entertained by TV with its constant noise and instant gratification, we're not called on to use our imaginations, to interact or react. We just lie there, numb and mindless.

We've done exactly what Socrates feared—we've lost our memories, forgotten our stories, turned away from the very thing that binds us together in our humanity.

Madeleine Stowe, when asked about Sean Connery, her costar in the movie *Playing by Heart*, said she was most taken by his ability to tell stories.

"He has complete recall of his past, his childhood. How is that we've all forgotten how to tell stories the way he can? It's become a lost art."

Artists are today's storytellers. Whether their stories are told in paintings, in films, or in bedtime reveries, artists keep the history of their tribe. They pass down traditions, define the time in which they live.

Don't you have a story to tell?

INVENT A NEW BOARD GAME

The Games Gang

Don't laugh. Rob Angel was a waiter until he came up with the board game Pictionary, which, in the first six months of national distribution, sold five million copies. Maybe you want to make up a murder mystery game complete with characters who end up being suspects. A unique game that only your family plays. Invite your friends over and kick some ideas around.

Design a garden.

Make a paper doll of your first
boyfriend/girlfriend.

Have a fifteen-minute conversation
with your body.

You're in Good Company

Richard Bach's 10,000-word story about a soaring
seagull was rejected eighteen times before Macmillan
finally published it in 1970. By 1975, it had sold more
than seven million copies in the United States alone.

Week
Twenty-seven

I always said I wanted to be somebody.
I guess I should have been more specific.

LILY TOMLIN

THE PEARL OF FAILURE

World War I was over and Walt Disney, who had joined the Red Cross ambulance corps by forging his parents' signature, had a dream. So what if he was only eighteen, a kid compared to the rest of the staff at *The Kansas City Star*?

His burning ambition, the dream that kept him going through long, tedious days chauffeuring boisterous colonels around France and delivering beans and sugar to military hospitals, was the thought of a cartoonist job at his hometown newspaper, *The Kansas City Star*.

He'd already thrown newspapers for the venerable publishing company, getting up every morning at 3:30 to neatly roll and prepare the morning news for eager readers. Each dawn, as he leafed through the paper, admiring the drawings of the cartoonists who graced the editorial pages, he'd think, "Someday that will be me."

Now that he was back from the war, surely the *Star* would be happy to hire such an up-and-coming artist.

He gathered his portfolio, barged into the office of the newspaper's employment director, and waited, pen poised, to sign his W-4s. But instead of the "welcome aboard" that he had set his sights on, the kindly gentleman said, "Sorry, we can't use you."

Talk about defeat. Disney's highest aspiration had just been ground into little pieces. Everything he'd worked for, been dreaming of had just flown out the window.

How was he to know then that life had something bigger in store?

If he had been like most of us, he would have retreated, tail between his legs, into the basement. He'd have listened to that voice that haunts all of us, that voice that taunts, "See, I told you you were no good."

He could have listened to that voice again when, a few months later, Pressman-Rubin Studios, an ad agency that hired him to draw farm equipment, laid him off after one short month because of his "singular lack of drawing ability."

Sure, it took him a while to lick his wounds, but by the time he was twenty-one, he was using that same "lack of drawing ability" to create Laugh-O-Grams, animated reels of Kansas City residents and buildings interspersed with news headlines, public service announcements, and jokes told by Disney's first animated character, Professor Whosis. Shown in Kansas City movie theaters before the main feature, Laugh-O-Grams were popular enough that Disney was able to hire animators (he offered "free animation lessons" to anyone interested in the cartoon business) to join him in the family garage.

Disney's dream began to grow bigger. He wanted to reach an audience larger than Kansas City, to create a cartoon that would appeal to a national distributor. Writing a simple adaptation of "Little Red Riding Hood" and shooting it entirely with his single hand-cranked camera, he talked the general manager of the chain of theaters that showed Laugh-O-Grams into sending prints to New York distributors. Every major distributor said no. The one small company that liked it enough to send a one-hundred-dollar advance proceeded to go belly up within a month.

By 1923, even though he'd received five hundred dollars for a short called *Tommy Tucker's Tooth* that was produced for a local dentist, and received an encouraging letter from a New York–based independent distributor interested in seeing his proposed *Alice in Wonderland*, Disney's five newly hired animators had quit, and Laugh-O-Grams had collapsed into insolvency.

Another defeat. Another failure.

So next time your dreams hit a dead end, think of Walt Disney. Realize that maybe the reason your dreams aren't coming true is because they're not quite big enough yet.

Maybe your vision is ahead of its time and the playing field you're suiting up for isn't grand enough to hold you.

The only thing failure says is "Try again somewhere else."

We're the only ones that interpret "no" to mean "Give up," "It's too late," "You're the scourge of the universe."

"No" just means that God has a bigger plan.

It wasn't until Disney hocked his movie camera for a forty-dollar train fare to California that his dreams really started to come true. He thought making it as a *Kansas City Star* cartoonist would give him everything he needed.

Had he met his "highest" dreams, the *Star* would have had a so-so editorial cartoonist, a guy none of us would have ever heard of. I wouldn't have just taken my daughter to see *Tarzan*, the thirty-seventh animated feature in the Disney lineup. There would be no Mickey Mouse, no *Lady and the Tramp*, no Disneyland. My friend Kitty would never have been able to do her Donald Duck imitation.

All I can say is thank goodness Walt Disney was a failure.

DRAW THREE VERSIONS OF A GIRAFFE

Stick Your Neck Out

Yes, there's always a stick version. Here are a couple of mine. But how about a watercolor giraffe or a pointillist giraffe? By the way, do giraffes have spots?

More Fun Stuff

Practice a new walk.

Perfect some animal noise.

Tape paper to the TV and write down ideas for your own TV shows.

You're in Good Company

When actor Hugh Grant was in a slump, he decided to write a novel. Every day, he'd go to the London Library to write. "I used to write something in the morning and think, 'I'm a genius,' then go out for a chicken sandwich and come back and throw it away," he said.

WEEK 28

It is obvious that most
people come to know
only one corner of their
room, one spot near the
window, one narrow
strip on which they keep
walking back and forth.   RAINER MARIA RILKE

PLATO SAID IT BEST: KNOW THYSELF

If you really knew who you were, you'd never have reason to doubt yourself. But unfortunately, most of us are so busy conforming to some weird ideals we inherited from our parents or our second-grade teacher that we've forgotten who we really are.

It's important to claim your life as your own. Most of us don't. We're too busy keeping up with the Joneses, wearing the perfume that Calvin Klein told us to wear, or listening to the music that Dick Clark or some Top Forty chart said we should like. This is where the real you got buried.

You've probably heard that cliché "Get a life." But that's the whole point of this book: to find out who you really are. To honor that special person.

And while getting rid of fear and old programming is important, that's only part of the picture. Remember, since thoughts are things and what we focus on expands, it's important to concentrate on who you want to be. Sure, you learn about yourself by digging up old skeletons from your past. But you also learn about yourself by figuring out who your favorite baseball player is or telling someone your secret dream.

Today's self-help books talk about owning your childhood and healing past hurts. Sure, your inner child was wounded by your parents, but he also dreamed of magic and made castles out of sand. Let's get to know this inner child. Why spend a lot of time working out the depressed, yucky part of you? The inner magician is just as real, just as present.

Another problem with owning your own life is today's pervasive mass media. We all watch the same exact TV shows and read the same exact newspapers with stories from the same exact news bureaus.

You probably know what your favorite movie is or maybe who your favorite movie star is, but what about your favorite constellation?

In the old days, each person drew upon the strength within himself and he didn't listen to the mass media for answers. He didn't need a critic to tell him if a movie was good or a painting was valuable. He had no doubt who he was.

Maybe you already know the answers to the following questions. If so, you've undoubtedly discovered the richness of your own life. Congratulations. Go ahead and move on to next week's lesson if you want to.

Unfortunately, however, most of us don't know. We've never sat down long enough to think about anything uniquely important to us.

A couple of pointers: If you can't think of an answer, do a little research. Maybe you'll have fun finding out who your favorite president was. Maybe you'll learn so much about the American political system that you'll end up running for mayor and changing your entire life. Feel free to write one word, a paragraph, or a whole book. Maybe the person you are will end up on the best-seller list.

Ready, set, go.

1. Speaking of stars, what is your favorite constellation?

2. When was your first visit to the doctor?

3. What sport would you like to be good at?

4. What's your favorite city? If it's the one you're in, describe it to someone. What do you like about it? Maybe it's the Polish breadmaker down the street. Or the fact that all your cousins live there. Or because the magnolia trees are gorgeous in the spring. Have you really thought about this?

5. What's your favorite building in town?

6. Who is your favorite poet? You don't know? This is where the library card will come in handy. If you don't know, go find out. And remember, songwriters like the Indigo Girls and Bob Dylan are modern-day poets.

7. What's your favorite river? Tree? Flower? Don't forget to ask yourself why you like these things. It will reveal great truths to you.

8. What are you good at? Don't forget things like building friendships or making banana bread. Maybe you're exceptionally good at keeping the peace. Or making others feel good about themselves.

9. What's your favorite color?

10. What was your favorite book as a kid?

11. Who was your favorite president? Is that library card burning in your pocket?

12. What's your favorite letter? Number? Era? Planet?

13. In the movie *The Way We Were*, Robert Redford and his friend spend an enjoyable day naming their favorite day.

158

Favorite year? Favorite age? Also, what was your favorite grade in school? Why?

14. What would you name a boat if you owned one?

15. Who was your favorite cartoon character when you were a child?

16. What is your nickname? What nickname would you like to have? What would you nickname a coworker?

17. What's your favorite card game?

18. What movie would you like to see made?

19. What does an angel look like?

20. Who is your hero?

21. What do you think of questions like these? Why?

Now that you've come up with the answers, do you see a thread running through them? Have you discovered anything about yourself?

159

WRITE A SCENE FROM YOUR NEW SCREENPLAY

Lights, Camera, Action

What? You haven't started your screenplay? Okay, here's all you have to do. Remember that character you made up a few weeks ago? Put him in an elevator. Make up another character. He, too, steps in the elevator. Only problem is the elevator sticks between the third and fourth floors. What happens?

Name an angel.

Create a "drama" and call Dr. Laura to
find out what to do.

Design a birdhouse.

You're in Good Company

Teachers of opera singer Enrico Caruso said he had
no voice at all and could not sing. His parents encouraged him to be an engineer.

Week 29

CATCHING THE GLOW

When Oprah hosted Richard Gere in October 1997, she asked him why he practiced Buddhist meditation. He thought about it for a minute, took a deep breath, and gave this answer: "It clears the air of low-flying clouds that block the glow."

He could have just as easily been talking about the spiritual practice of art. Art is a powerful way to tap the higher consciousness, to see the glow that's blocked, as Gere said, by the low-flying clouds.

Inside you are deep, wide, unfathomable dimensions. By serving any discipline of art you cast a rod into this bottomless mystery and bring up something that is normally beyond your reach. Someone described this other world as a stage magician's trunk. Although it's not apparent to the naked eye, the trunk has a trap door and secret drawers.

You can no more escape the pull of this magic than you can the pull of gravity. It's what makes us respond to the birth of a kitten, the thunder rattling the stars, the death of an old withered maple.

Art has transformational powers not just for the individuals who practice it but for society as a whole. Every time one person increases the spiritual voltage, all of us see more clearly.

To practice art—be it to chip a statue, to arrange flowers, to write a situation comedy—is to affirm meaning, to say yes to God despite all the tragedy and ambiguities that surround us.

There's a strong sentiment afoot (thank you, Jesse Helms) that the arts are frosting, frou-frou, expendable, unnecessary. This is the same voice that tells you you're expendable, the voice that assigns you a number, a punch card, a place in line. It's the voice of the ego, the voice that's desperately afraid you're going to figure it out.

The other voice, the magical voice, is the voice that calls you to be more, the voice for God.

Art then is nonviolent resistance, resistance to the dog biscuits that society wants to throw you so you'll speak, sit, and roll over.

Usually, when we aspire to "be spiritual," we think of things like being kinder, being more understanding, saying more prayers.

But in order to really fulfill our destiny as spiritual beings, we must also become more creative, more open to the magic, the deep vistas that gush through our souls.

A true artist is simply a prism that reflects God's light. Most artists readily admit their art comes from somewhere outside themselves. It's somehow bigger than they are.

Songwriter Phoebe Snow called herself a vessel. She said she had no idea who wrote "Poetry Man," her big hit of the '70s. When people ask her what she was thinking when she wrote it, she says, "I have to tell them I really don't know. It doesn't have anything to do with me."

163

It came to her from someplace else.

Spirit is just as eager to shine through you. All you have to do is raise your hand. If you devote yourself to creativity, spirit will answer. Spirit is always recruiting people who are willing, folks who will show up for this mystical, magical electricity that constantly beckons.

It's there. The only real question is, When are you going to plug it in?

MAKE A SCULPTURE

Henry Moore or Less

You've already mastered balloon sculpting. Feel free to make another one, but maybe by now you'd like to move to another medium—maybe Popsicle sticks or Play-Doh. I once made a sculpture of George Washington from a used oatmeal container. Okay, so I was only in fifth grade, but nevertheless, it was a sculpture. Maybe you're ready for papier-mâché or bronze. It's up to you.

More Fun Stuff

Write the acceptance speech for
your Oscar.

Design a logo.

Have "hat night" at dinner.

You're in Good Company

"I react psychologically the way other people react
when the plane loses an engine. It's really scary just
getting to the desk," says Fran Lebowitz.

WEEK
30

I do wish to run, to seize this greatest time in all the history of man
to be alive, stuff my senses with it, eye it, touch it, listen to it,
smell it, taste it, and hope that others will run with me,
pursuing and pursued by ideas and idea-made machines.

RAY BRADBURY

CELEBRATING LIFE

How long has it been since you've danced? Be honest now. I'm
talking about really dancing, where the beat and your body become one. Where you surrendered to the rhythm and lost all sense
of time.

Okay, so when was the last time you sang a song? Or skipped?
Or laughed, for that matter?

In *Divine Secrets of the Ya-Ya Sisterhood*, the Ya-Yas, four life-
long friends, survive divorce, alcoholism, even death by using
humor and a sense of joy in the details of their lives. In the whole
scheme of things, their lives are pretty ordinary. None of them are
famous or have earth-shattering careers. None of them are millionaires or even known outside their little burg of Thornton, Al-
abama. But boy, do those ladies know how to live! They turn these

ordinary lives into something extraordinary. They don't just fix dinner, they make a feast. They don't just throw parties, they host galas. Everything they attempt is done with aplomb.

That's what being creative is all about. It's more than just making a painting or submitting a poem. It's about making a life.

Look up the word *creativity* in the dictionary and you'll find a picture, to borrow an old Rodney Dangerfield joke, of my friend Michelle. She doesn't write (except for Christmas cards in January) or paint, but everything she does is done with joie de vivre, a sense of sparkle. In her kitchen, for example, she posted a picture of a fierce dragon with these words: "Mom without coffee." She stages a Monty Python film festival every February, makes costumes that RuPaul would sell his implants for, and throws parties where everyone comes naked except for raincoats.

She's a kindred spirit to Dame Edith Sitwell, who said, "I am not eccentric. I'm just more alive than most people. I am an electric eel in a pond of goldfish."

The vast majority of adults in this country have become goldfish. They've turned their joy thermostats way down. Having fun is just too much trouble. They're trying to save energy. What they don't realize is joy and fun actually create energy.

Next time you're at an airport, notice what happens when a flight gets canceled. Children barely notice. They just keep on playing hopscotch, singing, "I love you, you love me, we're a happy fam-o-ly," and crawling under their seats. Only their seats are not seats. They're ghost houses or castles or magic playrooms.

Adults just sit there, looking at their watches and then looking at them again in five minutes.

Every day, we have 1,440 minutes. We can either waste those precious minutes looking at our watches or we can turn ourselves into electric eels.

WRITE A POEM
ON A PARK SIDEWALK

Take a Poet to the Park

Yes, it would be nice if this was a poem of your own making, but if not, find a poem that speaks to your soul and put it out there to talk to someone else's soul. A phone-repair man in Kansas City uses different-colored chalk to write his poems at Loose Park. He goes late at night when no one is there and leaves beautiful sentiments for people who come the next day.

ROSES ARE RED
VIOLETS ARE BLUE
I HEARD WHAT YOU SAID
AND I LOVE YOU TOO!

Put on your favorite CD and dance for
fifteen minutes.

Buy a lottery ticket and compose a plan
for how you'd spend the winnings.

Stage a story time.

You're in Good Company

Whatever works!! John Cheever used to put on his
business suit, leave his apartment, and go to his
basement, where he hung his suit on a hanger and
wrote in his underwear. Henrik Ibsen hung a picture of August Strindberg, his mortal enemy, near
his writing desk. Friedrich von Schiller couldn't
write unless his bare feet were immersed in cold water, rotting apples were in his desk-side cupboard,
and a red curtain was drawn. Jack Kerouac wrote
by candlelight.

Write down all the things you can't do, all the things that keep you from following your dream.

1.
2.
3.
4.
5.
6.
7.
8.
9.
10.
11.
12.
13.
14.
15.
16.
17.
18.
19.
20.
21.

Now then, tear out this page and burn it.

GET DOWN AND DIRTY

The first thing we need to do is change our terminology. This book is not going to encourage you to create art. Instead, we're going to "make stuff."

And here's why: Art has too much baggage. It's pretentious and intimidating. It makes you feel like you should stand up straight and mind your manners.

Look at most art museums. Not only are they huge structures with big columns and cavernous lobbies, but they're filled with stern guards who dress like policemen and give you dirty looks if you so much as cough in the wrong direction. The art is sealed tightly behind glass. You can't get close enough to breathe on it, let alone touch it with your grubby little paws.

Art museums seem to set up a kind of us-against-them mentality. We're the peons who pay to look at the art. The geniuses

thirty-one

week

who create it were old guys from Europe who liked to cut off their body parts.

And if there's anything that's 100 percent effective at bringing up unresolved insecurity issues, it's first-of-the-month Friday night art gallery openings. You have to dress really "cool," preferably in something black, refrain from smiling, and, if at all possible, make your hair do something gymnastic. If you do say anything (my tactic is usually not to speak, making people believe I'm deep in profound thought), it had better be brilliant. I always feel like I'm an impostor, that I'm not—no matter how "hip" I pretend to be—ever going to fit in with the "beautiful people" of the art world.

So that's why I like the idea of "making stuff." It kicks pretense out the door. None of us in our fragile states as budding "stuff makers" need anything to do with approval. Forget Pauline Kael. Forget whether some snobbish art critic who probably reviews art only because he's too petrified to make his own likes it or not. We're simply making stuff. Every week, we're going to make something different—a poem, a song, a character.

But just remember it's only stuff.

My favorite art has always been made by what the art world calls "folk artists" or "outside" artists. Using whatever material is handy—tree trunks, old refrigerator doors, broken bottles— these poor, often rural folks who can neither read nor write just one day started whittling or stacking or painting. In other words, making stuff. Not only have few of them ever heard of Monet or van Gogh, but most of them have had little schooling of any kind.

Howard Finster, a retired Baptist minister who didn't pick up a paintbrush until he was in his sixties, had a sixth-grade education. One day, God says to him, "Howard, I want you to start painting." He quickly reminded God that he had no clue how to paint, and God retorted just as quickly, "How do you know?" That was 1973 and, at last count, he had made 44,500 paintings. Of course, he also likes to paint accordions, lawn mowers, oxygen pumps, and telephones. Art? you're asking. Just ask Robin Williams, Barbra Streisand, Andy Williams, Bill Cosby, Woody Allen, and other fans who have paid upward of $20,000 for his artwork. Unpretentious? You bet. He makes all of his stuff from his vibrating bed in Summerville, Georgia.

In the old days, everybody made everything. If you wanted a new dress, you made it yourself. If the family dinner table wore out, you chopped down a tree and hauled it to the barn, where the lathe and the wood shop were set up. There were no grocery stores and even if there had been, there weren't cars to take you there. You grew your own food, wove your own wall hangings, built your own house. Today, when someone says they built their own house, they mean that they bought blueprints from an architect they found in the phone book and hired craftsmen to "do the dirty work."

This is what we want to do: the dirty work. This dirty work is what feeds us, what connects us to our true natures. When we let other people make all our things, we lose a piece of who we really are. We cut ourselves off from our source. By making things, we tap into a prolific wellspring that literally grows us into masters.

Even those of us who still cook our own food and weave our own wall hangings have turned over our Friday and Saturday night entertainment to the experts. We go to the movies, rent videos, listen to CDs. It doesn't even occur to us to write our own scripts, sing our own songs. A hundred years ago there was no *ER* on Thursday nights, no *X-Files* on Sunday nights—so if the family wanted to celebrate the end of a long day, they sat down and told stories or made up a song on the family guitar.

Art? Nah, they were just making stuff.

COME UP WITH TWO IDEAS FOR TV SITCOMS

Call Your Agent

Now that Jerry Seinfield has retired and *Mad About You* is off the air, there's plenty of room for new sitcoms.

I've always wanted to do a sitcom set at an intentional community—you know, what most people call a commune. Not only are there lots of characters (I met a very handsome man at one who often wore a skirt), but these characters live together in tight situations, making interesting plots inevitable.

More Fun Stuff

Invite all your friends to watch the
sunset. Hold up cards (1 to 10) to rate
the "show."

Celebrate the birthday of your
favorite writer.

Go to a movie dressed in costume
(à la *Rocky Horror Picture Show*.)

You're in Good Company

SARK ate ketchup sandwiches for years before she
finally made it as an artist/author.

177

Week 32

You might as well fall flat on your face as lean over too far backwards.

JAMES THURBER

Thank God, the public only sees the finished product.

WOODY ALLEN

ART DIVINERS

We idolize Picasso, enter radio contests to go backstage with Bon Jovi, write fan mail to Leonardo DiCaprio, and yet we don't give the time of day to the Picassos and Bon Jovis within our own homes.

That lady in the grocery store with the three screaming kids has a funny poem in her heart. The accountant with the alligator briefcase has a rock video in his head. The video clerk with the purple hair has an original screenplay under the counter.

The people you walk by every day have untold talents, passions that beat in their chests like a witch doctor's drum.

But we're so busy watching the "real" artists on *Entertainment Tonight* that we don't even notice.

How many Barbra Streisands, Robert Motherwells, Laurence Oliviers do you already know? The guy you sleep beside every night, the woman who packs your lunch every morning has powerful yearnings and stories and songs. And yet we yawn and ask if they've seen our brown socks. Instead of asking our loved ones to dance, we ask them to take out the trash.

Could it be we're asking the wrong questions?

Everywhere around us are people like John Suta, a seventy-six-year-old retired pipe fitter from Eugene, Oregon, who despite heart problems and nerve damage in his legs shows up every day with his tarnished French horn to practice with the Roosevelt Middle School band; people like Keith Anderson, a marketing manager from Westwood Hills, Kansas, who three times a week heads to a tiny workshop in his basement to blend fibers and dyes to make paper.

The call for magic beckons to all of us like steam rising from a fresh-baked pie.

Yet we still think Martin Scorsese, Mozart, and Julia Roberts are the ones who drew the lucky straws.

If professional artists did draw a straw that was different from yours or mine, it's only the straw of being born in the right place at the right time.

If Mozart had not been born in eighteenth-century Salzburg to a father who led the local orchestra, he might not have started composing.

If Matisse had been born in, oh say, Sandusky, Ohio, it's unlikely he'd have become the artist he did. On the other hand, if Leroy Watkins had been born in Le Cateau in 1869, his paintings might be seducing the big spenders today.

Renoir, Monet, Cézanne, Pissarro, Degas, and the other Impressionists who we now hail as geniuses became geniuses only because they stoked those fires. They didn't ask, "Where are my brown socks?" They wanted to know how far they could go in capturing light and shadow, in recording the pleasures of their every-

179

day lives. They became allies, sharing studio space and taking painting excursions together. They supported one another and nurtured this new "life form."

Like the Impressionists, we have the power to make the place and time the right ones. We can stoke our genius, band together, nurture the art inside our brothers.

Wouldn't it be great to be able to say my town, Winfield, Kansas, or Lewistown, Montana, was the birth of some new art form? And why couldn't it be?

Motown didn't exist because all the musical talent was born in Detroit in the 1950s and '60s. It existed because one man decided to mine the talent that was there. He could have just as easily looked in Denver, Colorado.

Maybe the most important task any of us could undertake is to become a diviner of art, to take a willow switch and feel for the deep artistic vein that coils and creeps within our brothers, the vein that whispers, "You could be more."

WRITE A THREE-LINE PITCH FOR THE MOVIE YOU'RE GOING TO WRITE

Terminator Meets *Terms of Endearment*

In Hollywood, movies have been made solely on a pitch. You've got the studio's ear for three minutes (if you're lucky), so you have to be able to pitch it quick and fast. What's yours?

Do mime on a street corner.

Go shopping in Groucho Marx
nose and glasses.

Ride up and down in an elevator
all day and draw shoes.

You're in Good Company

James Joyce couldn't start writing each morning
until he'd smoked a half pack of cigarettes and con-
sumed mass quantities of coffee. Finally, after all
that, he said, there was no further excuse.

WEEK
thirty-three

The role of the artist is not to find solutions, but to compel us to love life in all its countless, inexhaustible manifestations.

LEO TOLSTOY

OH, THE THINKS YOU CAN THINK

Dr. Seuss wrote forty-seven books, won three Academy Awards, and landed the prestigious Pulitzer Prize.

But to the day of his death at age eighty-seven, he maintained that his incredible success was "mostly luck." His first children's book, *And to Think That I Saw It on Mulberry Street*, was rejected by twenty-seven publishers. They thought it was "too different," "didn't have a moral or a message."

At thirty-two, Ted Geisel ("Dr. Seuss" was a pen name he manufactured in college) decided his quest to publish a book was futile. He marched out of the office of that twenty-seventh publisher with a firm conviction that the only sensible thing to do was head to his apartment and stage a ceremonial burning of the manuscript that he'd worked on for so long.

As he strode grimly down Madison Avenue, his head down, he was hailed by an old friend from college.

"Hey, what's that under your arm?" asked Mike McClintock, the friend who had been a year behind him at Dartmouth.

Dejectedly, Geisel told him it was nothing, just a book he was going home to burn.

McClintock, who had three hours earlier been appointed juvenile editor of Vanguard Press, said, "Hey, we're standing outside my office. Let's go up and look at it."

Within a half hour, a contract was signed, leading to Geisel's longtime belief in luck.

He always said, "If I had been going down the other side of Madison Avenue, I'd be in the dry-cleaning business today."

Was it luck? I prefer to think Geisel's chance meeting with an old college buddy was a near-perfect example of Louis Pasteur's famous credo, "Fortune favors the prepared mind."

Geisel had mastered his scales. He'd been drawing since he was a kid, penciling cows with angel wings, dogs crossing tightwires, and chickens with windmills for tails in the margins of his school notebooks.

Even after his first success, he continued to work hard—seven days a week, in fact, while he was dreaming up *The Lorax*, *Horton Hears a Who*, or one of his many other children's classics.

Geisel called it luck. I call it synchronicity. When you make the commitment to really learn your song, a whole choir of angels and a twenty-piece orchestra will sign on to accompany you.

At a Salt Lake City writers' conference, Geisel said the best piece of advice he could dispense was "Write a verse a day, not to send to publishers, but to throw in wastebaskets."

He also counseled young artists to "paint at least one picture a month that is just for fun."

In other words, practice, practice, practice.

Jay Leno says it's like lifting weights. You've got to do it every day. You don't have to set aside hours, but do a little something every single day. Write a haiku (how hard can seventeen syllables

ART AND SOUL

be?) or make up a jingle for a product you use. Draw a new hat for the Cat in the Hat.

Just like the bicep that gets bigger with every pump of the iron, our creativity and imagination work better when they are exercised. The even better news is that your mind is so eager to perform its inherent function that it will shape up a heck of a lot faster than a tennis swing or a volleyball serve, which are not inherent human talents.

It's important to put creativity on your priority list. You wouldn't think of going a day without brushing your teeth or taking a shower. Isn't the unfoldment of your dreams at least as important?

When you give your creativity a daily workout, your imagination is armed and ready to take on any challenge.

Green Eggs and Ham, for example, was a "challenge" that, given to the imagination, reaped big benefits. It all started one day in Mexico when Geisel's publisher, Bennett Cerf, bet him fifty dollars that he couldn't write a book using just fifty words.

"You're on," Geisel said, and proceeded to deliver a manuscript to the Random House office on April 19, 1960. It went on to sell tens of millions of copies and still ranks as his most popular book.

The Cat in the Hat, another best-selling book, was also written with a challenge to Geisel's imagination. William Spaulding, head of educational publishing at Houghton Mifflin, wanted a book for six- and seven-year-olds who had already mastered the basic mechanics of reading. Studies at the time bemoaned the growing literacy problem, and Spaulding wanted something lively and fun that would entice young readers to read. He gave Geisel 225 words.

"I read the list forty times and got more and more frustrated," he recalls. "There were no adjectives. It was like making strudel without any strudels."

Out of desperation, he read it one more time and decided he'd give the first two words that rhymed to his imagination.

Needless to say, he found the word *cat* and then *hat* and his imagination took it from there.

Do you have a challenge that's particularly baffling? Give it to the imagination. Take your shoes off. Put your feet up. Let your imagination do the work.

CREATE A COMIC STRIP CHARACTER

See You in the Funny Pages!

Poor Charlie Brown! His kite is always getting stuck in a tree, his advice-giving friend Lucy has the gall to charge him five cents, and his dog Snoopy thinks he's the Red Baron. What character could you create?

Maybe there's somebody from your life. Look at Cathy Guisewite, who was an ad hack until she created *Cathy*, who speaks for a whole generation of single female baby boomers.

More Fun Stuff

Stage a charades party.

Celebrate the full moon.

Draw your fairy godmother.

You're in Good Company

Blake Edwards took a seven-year sabbatical when a script was taken away from him because his view on the project was different than the "star's" view.

She lacked nerve.
You've got to have nerve.

GEORGIA O'KEEFFE

DOING IT FAST

Fifty minutes was all it took—from conception to
the final applause. The Singles Group at the Village Presbyterian Church in Prairie Village, Kansas, wrote, produced, and starred in "The Dare
to Be Mediocre, Really Awful, Really Wonderful
Variety Show."

When they walked in at 6:30, they thought
they were coming to hear a speaker, maybe hit on
the cute blonde in the second row. Boy, were they
surprised when I passed out assignments and told
them they would be conducting the workshop
themselves.

First, each participant got a name—Billy
Crystal, Garth Brooks, Mikhail Baryshnikov, Tom
Cruise, and so on. There were fifteen names in
all, fifteen groups that had twenty minutes to get
together and create an act that would then be per-
formed in front of the rest of the group. The Mikhail Baryshnikovs, for example, had to choreo-
graph and perform a dance.

It happened so fast they didn't have time to
conjure up excuses or remember that they don't
know how to write a poem.

189

I gave them three rules.

1. Don't think.

2. Don't judge.

3. Just do.

And then, of course, I gave them the number-one rule that's most important every time you create anything:

> You have permission to fail, to be mediocre, to suck sewer slime.

But, but . . .

"But I don't want to be Placido Domingo. I want to be Walt Whitman."

"That's okay," I told them. "This is the time to stretch yourself, to try new things."

But, but . . .

"This is stupid," some of them protested.

I told them simply to notice their reactions ("I could never do that," "I'm not good enough," "I can't paint," "I'm scared," etc.) and told them to join the club. Everybody thinks they're not good enough.

I pointed out that:

- Goldie Hawn was once a go-go dancer and made ten dollars a night.

- Clint Eastwood was a busboy.

- Willie Nelson was a church choir director.

- Barbara Bush, in her recent biography, said, "I was so shy. I once cried over having to speak to the Houston Garden Club."

Everybody, I said, has to start somewhere.

I also told them that their resistance shows them an area of their lives that they've shut down and, if nothing else, it offers good insight into how they approach life.

Then I gave them their assignments. For example:

Placido Domingo

You are going to be a singer tonight. It doesn't matter if you've never sung in public. Tonight you have permission to sing a really awful song. Or maybe a good one. Sometimes, when we give ourselves permission to do things poorly, brilliance surfaces.

Think of songs you know—something from grade school like "Itsy Bitsy Spider" or "Twinkle, Twinkle, Little Star." I once sang "Sing, sing a song, sing out loud, sing out strong . . ." in front of a group. Yep, it's hard, but what do you have to lose? It will stretch you and grow you. Everybody pick a song and then have auditions among your group. Pick one or two people that will sing for the variety show.

Robin Williams

Yep, you are going to do some improvisation. Every person in your group will get a different character (the pile of characters will be waiting) and you are to act them out together. After ten minutes of improvising, pick two or three that will interact with each other during the variety show.

- a fifteen-year-old girl going on her very first date

- a lion

- the Statue of Liberty

- a dirty old man

191

- a gay poet

- an angry woman's libber

- a four-year-old

- a rooster

- a hungry dog

- a cowboy

- a coach

- a cavewoman

- the Taco Bell Chihuahua

Needless to say, some of them got up and left.

But those who stayed had a ball. The show, as they say, did go on. It wasn't Ziegfeld Follies or Barbra Streisand in Las Vegas. But it was real. And it was fun.

And, best of all, we all got to know one another. One lady who'd been coming to the group since her divorce three years ago told me she'd met more people that night than in all the other three years put together.

The guy who arranged the speakers asked me back. And I told him I would—just as soon as I finished this book.

GET OUT THE WATERCOLORS

Color your world!

I don't want to hear it. I don't care if you haven't painted since you were in fifth grade, I don't care that you don't own any watercolors. You can buy a children's set at Wal-Mart for $1.29. And you can paint on typing paper. Remember, we're in this for fun.

More Fun Stuff

Design an invitation to your first
sculpture show.

Rearrange your furniture.

Read *Random Acts of Kindness*.
Do three of them.

You're in Good Company

François Truffaut was a movie critic for years because he was too afraid to direct his own films.

WEEK 35

WRITE YOUR OWN BIBLE

My friend Greg Tamblyn, a talented songwriter, wrote a funny song that became the title of his first CD. It's called "Shoot-out at the I'm OK, You're OK Corral." It starts like this:

> *I could tell that it was more than just a simple lover's spat*
> *When she called me compulsive and blamed my mom for*
> *   that*
> *I yelled, "I'm not the only one with hang-ups, gal"*
> *And thus began the shoot-out at the I'm OK, you're OK*
> *   corral.*

It's funny because he and his girlfriend begin hurling insults at each other, lines they picked up from the latest self-help books. She says, "You've got the Peter Pan syndrome. You never grew up." And he returns with, "Looks who's talking? The Woman Who Loves Too Much."

It goes on to say:

195

I could tell she was going to fight me nail and tooth
When she brought up Dear Abby and quoted Dr. Ruth.

Although the song is hilarious, it touches a raw nerve. It points out one of the biggest problems in our culture. We don't turn inward. We're so busy quoting Dr. Ruth or Marianne Williamson or whomever the hottest new author happens to be that we forget to quote ourselves.

What do *we* think?

Most of us have no idea.

We look outside for answers. We look to everybody except ourselves.

And it's a shame. Life is being wasted. We're not having the fun that we could. We're not making the beautiful things that we could. We're not living, not celebrating, not polishing the unique jewels that each of us contains.

We're too busy cultivating the seven habits for highly effective people.

Why are we following rules that some author we've never met made up? I don't care how smart Suze Orman is, how together John Bradford is. They don't know the secrets to your life.

There's only one person who does.

What do you like? What is important to you?

Do you know?

An artist's first priority is to get acquainted with himself.

Only then can he sing his song.

You must recognize in yourself an individual, a new one, someone who's very distinct from the others. Find yourself. Find the fine thing that you are. Only then will you be liberated.

Looking to how-to books for answers blocks your own inner wisdom, thwarts the real answers. If you closed this book right now and started reading the instructions in your heart, you'd be brilliant within months.

This may come as a shock to you, but you have all the answers you will ever need. Nothing could be more enlightening than to have a frank talk with yourself.

Walt Whitman did this. His one great battle cry was for each man to find himself and then to give evidence of this uniqueness to the world.

"*Leaves of Grass*," he wrote, "has been an attempt from first to last, to put a person, a human being (myself in the latter half of the nineteenth century in America) freely, fully and truly on record."

He encourages each man to write his own Bible.

After you do that, you should write your own prayer. Make up your own credo. Dance to your own piper.

Why are the vast majority of adults in this country bored, lonely, and afraid?

Because they don't know who they are.

There are gigantic things that need to be done. Health care that needs to be reformed, education that needs to be improved. So many things could be made more beautiful.

How could anyone be bored?

We should be creating out of thrilling delight. We should live each day in vibrant exuberance. Our only job in this great big planet is to find our vitality, to discover what makes us want to jump on the table and dance.

Russell Conwell wrote a book in the late 1800s called *Acres of Diamonds*. It's about this guy named Ali Hafed who dedicates his life to finding the planet's biggest diamonds. He sells his home, leaves everything he knows, and sets out on a worldwide expedition to find record-setting gems. Finally, after years and years of fruitless trying, he comes back home, a spent and broken man. And guess what? The diamond, the big bad one that had eluded him, is right there in his own backyard.

COMPOSE A SONG

Sing, Sing a Song

If you don't have an instrument and don't want to make one, don't forget that thing in your mouth called a voice box. I know you can sing. Make something up on the spot. Or improvise. If "Grandma Got Run Over by a Reindeer" and a barking rendition of "Jingle Bells" can make it to the pop charts, what do you have to be embarrassed about?

My daughter's favorite song is one I made up called "Mom Loves Her Magical Tasman," and believe me, this kid has great taste.

Art Happens

Yes, it's a bumper sticker. Cut it out and put it on your car. How? you ask. You're creative. You'll figure it out.

(I pasted mine over a M.A.D.D. bumper sticker.)

More Fun Stuff

Go to a fancy hotel and put up a sign that says TAKE AN ARTIST TO LUNCH.

Wear two different shoes.

Build a sand castle.

You're in Good Company

E. B. White procrastinated by straightening every picture, every rug. He says, "Not until everything in the world is lined up perfectly true could anybody reasonably expect me to write."

After the president of Dartmouth College paid tribute to him for his "literary bravery," White thought, "He little knew." He later wrote to his wife that "the old emptiness and dizziness and vapors seized hold of me. Nobody who has never suffered my peculiar kind of disability can understand the sheer hell of such moments."

WEEK Thirty-six

A LITTLE HELP FROM OUR FRIENDS

When Judy Collins was a junior, a new English teacher came to East High School in Denver, where her family lived.

When the new teacher assigned the first paper, Judy eagerly chose to write about a play by T. S. Eliot that had deeply affected her. She was so excited about what she had written that she could barely sleep the night before she was to turn it in. She was convinced she would get an A.

Several days later, when all the papers were handed back except hers, she assumed the teacher was planning to read her essay to the class. Instead, when the bell rang, the teacher asked Judy to stay behind.

"Where did you get this?" the teacher demanded. "I don't believe you wrote this."

Even though the teacher was wrong and Collins' former teachers pleaded her case, showing papers that she had written before, assuring the new teacher that Judy was capable of this quality of writing, Judy felt so humiliated and guilty that she didn't write again for many years.

Unfortunately, Judy's story is all too common. A teacher or a parent or even society's all-too-familiar mantra that arts are a waste of time causes us to shut down a part of ourselves. We feel guilty for wanting to write poetry, wrong for liking to dance.

We're told not to color on the walls. To draw between the lines. To write about Alfred, Lord Tennyson even though we'd rather write about William Carlos Williams.

Better to follow the rules, step in line, do what the teacher says.

It's a wonder we get anything done at all.

Artists by their very nature are extremely sensitive. We want desperately for people to like us, to clap and to pat us on the back and say, "Good job."

But most times, they don't. They say, "no," "you can't," and "that's ridiculous." They think they're helping when they encourage us to "keep our day jobs."

But that doesn't mean you have to listen.

Collins finally gathered up the courage to listen to her heart, the voice that still knew how to write. But it took ten years, ten wasted years of feeling small and unworthy. Even though she was already a successful singer and had recorded a half dozen albums, she didn't feel good about writing again until she was twenty-seven, an entire decade after the teacher had accused her of plagiarism.

Luckily, she had some good friends.

Joni Mitchell, who had moved to New York about the same time Judy had, encouraged her to use some of the thoughts from her journals to write some songs.

Leonard Cohen said, "Hey, if I can write songs, so can you."

The neat part of this story is that Judy later helped Cohen, who was paralyzed by stage fright, to overcome it. She was appearing at a concert to raise money for the Vietnam War opposition and asked him to sing "Suzanne," the song he'd written that she'd made popular.

"I can't," he pleaded. "I'd die from embarrassment."

He got up halfway through the first verse and walked offstage. Judy wrapped her arms around him, put his guitar strap back on, and pointed him back toward the stage. He pulled back his shoulders, marched back on stage, finished "Suzanne," and has been giving concerts ever since.

To this day, Collins thinks it's very important to be around people with an artistic vision.

I'd have to say I agree. We all need comrades who can hold the high watch for us, who can say "Bravo" when we want to say "I quit."

This myth of the lonely, long-suffering artist exacts a high price. We don't have to be alone and, in fact, many times can create even better when we peek out of our isolated artist's garrets to say, "Hi!"

Despite what you may have heard, artists *are* social animals. From time immemorial they've gathered in cafés to share ideas, grouse about editors, trade tips on the best place to buy paint. Hemingway's little black book included Gertrude Stein, F. Scott Fitzgerald, Matisse, and many other well-known artists.

Maxine Kumin and Anne Sexton, both Pulitzer Prize–winning poets, had special phone lines installed in their homes so they could spend hours going over their work together. As fledgling poets, they first met at a poetry class at the Boston Center for Adult Education. They went on to form an informal poetry group that met twice monthly in members' homes.

Kumin's three children, when they saw her setting out the cups and glasses, always protested, "Oh no. Not the poets again. We'll never get any sleep."

They were probably right. When the chemistry's right, artists' get-togethers can get loud and exciting. One person's ideas inspires another's, and another's. Each contributes his or her piece to make something larger.

Within the first year, four of the five members of Kumin and Sexton's poetry group had published books.

Mary Shelley, who was barely twenty when she wrote *Frankenstein*, claimed she would never have come up with it if it weren't for a group of friends who whiled away summer hours at a Swiss resort by trying to best each other with ghost stories.

Pulitzer Prize winner Tony Kushner said the idea that he alone wrote *Angels in America* was pure rubbish. Actors, directors, former lovers, friends, and even one-night stands all left their traces in his play's text.

"It's fiction that artists labor in isolation and that artistic accomplishment is exclusively the provenance of individual talents," he said.

Art, rather than isolating us as it's so mythically portrayed, actually brings us together.

When we share our work, it binds us closer. We reveal ourselves to each other. When we read a poem or show a painting, we find kindred spirits, head-nodding friends who say, "Yeah, me too. That's just how I feel."

As Ralph Keyes says in *The Courage to Write*, this esprit "resembles neighbors battling a hurricane. Everyone is in equal jeopardy. Shared danger forges a bond."

So whomever you choose—a neighbor who loves to hear you sing, a famous writer you met at a writers' conference or a long-dead artist who comes to you in dreams and journals—find some support. Maybe Marx was right after all. The smallest divisible number is two, not one.

Fun Fact

Cathy Guisewite, creator of the popular *Cathy* comic strip, plugged college friend Lawrence Kasdan's movie *Grand Canyon* in her comic strip when it first came out.

MAKE AN INSTRUMENT

Music, Anyone?

You can make a drum from an old wastebasket or shakers with beans and empty soda pop bottles. Maybe you'll invent a new one like the Andean musicians who made shakers out of goat's toenails and a string instrument from an armadillo shell. Remember, anything is possible.

More Fun Stuff

Make a certificate (for best joke teller?? best sport??) and give it away.

Leave entertaining messages on friends' answering machines.

Get a book of spells from the library. Cast one.

You're in Good Company

Winning the Nobel Prize at age forty-four gave Albert Camus severe writer's block.

WEEK 37

Oh, Jane, face it. Everyone's got beans to spill.

ANN IN *THE COCKTAIL HOUR* BY A. R. GURNEY

HERE I AM

"Mommy, mommy, look at me!"

You probably haven't used that line in at least twenty years. But I guarantee you've wanted to, you've longed desperately for someone to hear you out. To notice you.

Joshua Kadison on his CD *Painted Desert Serenade* wrote a song called "The Invisible Man" about this guy who wakes up feeling a little uneasy, wonders if maybe he's disappearing.

He finally goes to the window, opens it, and yells at the top of his lungs, "Here I am! Here I am! Here I am!"

Although he's not really talking to anyone in particular, lights come on and people start yelling, "Will the crazy man go back to bed?"

He laughs, feeling better because someone heard what he said.

The song goes on to say, "It's no big thing. No revelation. No answer to these lives we lead. But I think I do know one thing.

Sometimes, we all need to say 'Here I am. Here I am. Here I am.' When life makes us feel like the invisible man."

That's what this book is really all about. Saying "Here I am." Saying "I count. I stand for something. I am not and never will be invisible."

All of us have so much to express. We have so many thoughts rolling around in our heads, so many boiling, seething dreams and plans.

But instead of expressing them, instead of saying, "Here I am," we buy a Hallmark card and let somebody else say it for us. When the people we most love graduate from high school, celebrate an anniversary, we rely on the "experts" at Hallmark to express our sentiments for this once-in-a-lifetime event. It's like multiple choice. Do I want to say what the lacy card with the flowers says or would I rather say what the blue plaid card says?

When we don't express ourselves, when we bottle up our angers, our fears, and our delights, we cut ourselves off from life's juice, from its joy.

It doesn't matter if you ever get published. It doesn't matter if you win an award or become really famous. What does matter is that you become willing and able to express who you are and how you feel.

You've got an entire world inside your head. At this point, it's like a cartoon door that doesn't come unlatched, but pulses around the edges while Wile E. Coyote or Bugs Bunny or some other character pushes on the door, spinning his legs, trying to keep it from coming open.

As Rollo May said in his landmark book *The Courage to Create*, "If you do not express your original ideas, if you do not listen to your own being, you will have betrayed yourself."

Instead of exploring and expressing the deep vistas of our minds, we settle for taking more in. We watch more TV, read more self-help books, see more movies.

209

In *The Library Card*, a brilliant children's book by Jerry Spinelli, a little girl named Brenda goes into shock when her parents decide to turn off the TV for a week. When a mysterious library card lures her to the library, she finds a book containing the story of her life, which ends abruptly on page fifteen with these words: "One day Brenda turned on the television."

Brenda didn't even know her favorite color. How many of us don't know our favorite color, our favorite anything?

How could we? We're too busy consuming.

It might be one thing if all the TV and books and movies were nourishing us. But we continue to get up from the table unsatisfied. Yeah, that movie was good, but isn't there something more?

There's always this gnawing feeling that something isn't right, something bigger and deeper and more satisfying is out there. But what? Where is it?

The only thing that can fully nourish you is your own self-expression. It cannot come from outside. It can come only from the soul of your being.

We all sense it's in there. That's why we feel uplifted when we see some beautiful painting or read a novel that speaks to our heart. It whispers to us, beckoning us like the scent of a freshly baked pie. C'mon, it says, bite me. You know you want to.

I believe that much of what we call depression is unclaimed creative expression. Instead of being released, our creative energy, our very life force is imploding on us.

We are *not* being who we are. We are not fulfilling our destinies. Instead, we're following rules that somebody else made up. We don't even know who *they* are—all we know is *they* told us to own a home and have a job and sire 2.5 kids.

When we don't create or express, we get homesick, homesick for ourselves. We're all dying of this homesickness, missing the richness, the beauty inside of us.

There's a chilling restaurant scene in the Monty Python film *The Meaning of Life* where an immense man saunters in and starts eating. And eating. One plate after another. Everybody in the restaurant stares in amazement. How can this guy keep taking this all in? Finally, when a waiter, played by John Cleese, insists he have just one more thin mint, the guy explodes and spews his insides all over the fancy, pretentious restaurant.

You don't want another thin mint. You just want to say, "Here I am."

Nyuk-Nyuk-Nyuk

Remember Larry,
Curley, and Moe with
his cereal-bowl
haircut? You might
want to hit yourself
in the head or stick
two fingers in your
eyes before you get
started. Get a pencil.
Ready, set, go.

More Fun Stuff

Make a papier-mâché piñata.

Paint a picture on a brown paper grocery bag.

Decorate a bicycle.

You're in Good Company

Three years after *The Great Gatsby* was published, F. Scott Fitzgerald had earned $5.15 in royalties. By the time he died, it was out of print.

WeeK 38

No question that there's an unconscious world. The problem
is how far is it from midtown and how late is it open?

WOODY ALLEN

FOCUS

One of the great metaphysical truths is that what you focus on expands. If you think about beauty, peace, and all the things you're grateful for, you'll see more beauty, peace, and things to be grateful for. If, on the other hand, you concentrate on all the lousy, good-for-nothing things that are happening to you, lousy, good-for-nothing things will continue to crop up like dandelions in a renting tenant's yard.

Sometimes it's hard to see the Oscar when you haven't so much as written the first "fade in." But you've got to hold it in your mind's eye. Forget the "facts"—the fact that you've never written a screenplay, the fact that you're not even sure how far to indent the first character's name.

Focus on that little gold statue sitting on your fireplace mantle. Focus on the applause as you go up to nervously give your acceptance speech.

Shirley Maclaine, who won an Oscar for best actress for her role as Aurora Greenway in *Terms of Endearment*, said she saw

214

herself getting an Oscar long before the March awards ceremony. She even pictured the dress she would wear.

As artists, we must always keep our eyes on the ball—not the ball that's apparent to the outer eye, but the ball that's calling us to another dimension. We must be willing to go places others won't dare.

Remember that Sunday afternoon when Jesus and his twelve disciples were out fishing? Jesus, who could bring up a week's supply of tuna in one lousy cast, probably got a little bored. Rather than sit there and twiddle his thumbs, he pops one leg over the side of the boat, pops over another, and starts walking toward the shore. On top of the water.

He wasn't swimming. He wasn't bobbing around in a rubber ring. He was walking on top of the water, something everyone "knows" you can't do.

You can imagine that his disciplines might have been a little disturbed.

Especially when Jesus hollers to them, "Anybody wanna come?"

"Not me," they all answer.

Except for one man.

It's a pretty sure bet that Jesus later named Peter as the rock on which his church would be built because he was the guy who was willing to get out of the boat.

He was willing to walk into a new experience, a new way of being. The rest of the disciples weren't ready. They clung to the boat.

That wouldn't have been so bad, but they nearly convinced Peter that he wasn't ready either.

As he confidently strode along the Red Sea, maybe even doing the Macarena as he went, his buddies started whispering among themselves.

"What a fool."

"He's going to sink."

"He'll never make it."

215

At that point, Peter had a choice. He could either listen to the old way. Or he could keep his focus on the new possibility.

Like all of us, he did take his eyes off the new possibility for a while. And, sure enough, he quickly started to sink.

Luckily, Peter was smart enough to look back up.

This is an important story for us as creators. First, we've got to be willing to try a new way of being. We've got to "get it" that we can walk on water, write a novel, sculpt a statue.

Peter was willing to believe that maybe a new experience was possible. He was willing to believe that he could step into the swirling sea and not sink.

As long as he kept his focus on that new possibility, he was fine. But the minute he pulled his focus back, started listening to the old way, he began to sink.

But the good news is that all he had to do was look back up, put his focus back on the new possibility.

You can tackle that project that everybody says you can't. You may sink from time to time. A little water in your nose won't hurt you.

Just be sure to keep looking back up.

Go ahead, get your feet wet.

COMPOSE THE TITLE
FOR YOUR DEBUT CD

A . . . B . . . CD

Hey, I didn't say you had to write the songs. All you have to do
is come up with a clever (maybe you prefer meaningful?) name
for the debut that will undoubtedly feature a
picture of you skipping down a beach
or lying in a hammock or
maybe playing
air guitar.

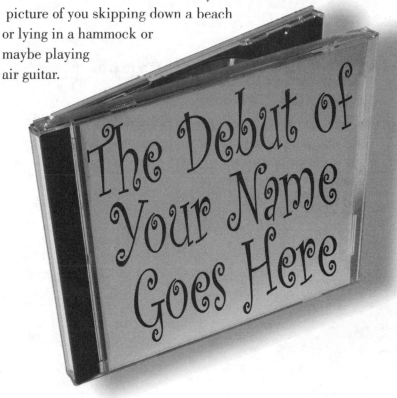

More Fun Stuff

Invent a new kind of pizza.

Buy a CD that hasn't made the pop charts.

Have a picnic at the park for breakfast.

You're in Good Company

Calvin Trillin calls his predraft a "vomit out," where he writes anything at all that comes to mind. He often worries that someone might see it before he gets around to cleaning it up.

ABRACADABRA

Most people associate the word *abracadabra* with magicians pulling rabbits out of top hats.

But the word *abracadabra* is actually an Aramaic term that translates into English as "I will create as I speak."

It's a powerful concept. It's why Edison often announced the invention of a device before he'd actually invented it.

It's why Jim Carrey wrote himself a check for $10 million long before he ever made a movie. Back when he was an unknown actor, he'd look at that check and think, "That will be mine someday." He didn't mention if he actually used the word *abracadabra*.

Turns out that what you say may not only be used against you in a court of law, but it may also be used *for* you once you come to realize that there's no such thing as idle words or idle thoughts.

When I first began writing for magazines, I had an inferiority complex that wouldn't have fit in Shea Stadium. Because I was from a small town in the Midwest, I couldn't imagine that I had

Week
Thirty-nine

anything to say to a fancy editor from New York. Although I sent query after query pitching my many ideas, I didn't really expect to sell too many. At best, I figured I could sneak a couple ideas under the cracks.

Needless to say, I got a lot of rejection letters, so many that I probably could have wallpapered the city of Cincinnati should they have needed wallpaper. The editors didn't exactly tell me to drop dead, but they didn't encourage me to keep writing either.

Then I read a book called *Write for Your Life* by Lawrence Block. In the early '80s, when his column for *Writer's Digest* magazine was at the height of its popularity, he and his wife, Lynn, decided to hold a series of seminars for writer-wannabes.

They called the day-long seminars "Write for Your Life" and set about booking hotel rooms in cities around the country. Unlike most writing seminars, where you learn to write plot treatments or how to get an agent, Block's seminar dealt with the only thing that really matters when it comes to being a writer: getting out of your own way. Getting rid of the countless negative thoughts that tell you what a hopelessly uninteresting specimen of humanity you are.

At the seminar, participants meditated, grabbed partners and confessed their greatest fears, and did all kinds of things that helped them get to the bottom of why they wanted to write, but didn't.

The seminars were hugely successful, but Block, who was a writer, not a seminar giver, eventually got tired of trotting around the country collecting tickets. Instead, he self-published the book that I ran into about the same time.

I took the book to heart. I did all of the exercises. I wrote affirmations. I consulted my inner child to find out what I was so afraid of. I even sent myself postcards for thirty days straight. On these postcards, I'd write such affirming reminders as "You, Pam, are a great writer." "You, Pam, have what it takes to sell to New York editors." "You, Pam, are interesting and people want to hear what you have to say."

220

I'm sure the mail carrier thought I was a little cracked, wasting 18 cents or whatever the postage was back then to send myself a postcard telling myself I was fascinating and abundant. But if he knew what a change it made in my life, he'd have been doing it, too.

Suddenly, I started getting assignments from the big national magazines with, yes, the big New York editors. This is probably a good time to mention that I have since met many of the New York editors and a great number of them are as insecure as me. Or as I used to be.

First, there was *Modern Bride*, which wanted a piece on exercises couples could do together. *Ladies' Home Journal* asked for a travel story on Tampa Bay. Suddenly, this once-insecure writer from Kansas was getting assignments from big national magazines, the kind of magazines you see in dentists' offices.

Did I suddenly start writing more fluidly, coming up with more compelling ideas? Probably a little bit (after all, that was one of my affirmations), but mostly I changed the reality of what I thought and said about myself.

I'd like to tell you this realization has permanently changed my life.

It hasn't. I still feel insecure and unworthy a lot of the time.

But I now know that, like the magician, I can keep pulling rabbits out of top hats, playing cards out of sleeves, and bouquets of flowers out of white handkerchiefs. I just have to say and believe that it's true.

DYE
SOCKS
AND
T-SHIRT
TO
MATCH

Dye
Laughing

Remember
tie-dye?
Dying things
is a good
reminder that
if you don't like
something,
you have the
power to
change it.

More Fun Stuff

Eat all your meals outside today.

Get up at 3 A.M. to see what's on television.

Go to a deserted field and dance.

You're in Good Company

Phil Collins was convinced that after *Face Value* he was all dried up.

I was taught that prayer, like good manners,
consisted of "please" and "thank you."

ADRIANA DIAZ

GLORY TO GOD

"Now I lay me down to sleep . . ."

I must have droned that line ten thousand times.

Always the good little girl, I rotely recited my prayers like a Weed Eater devouring hedges. Before meals, there was "God is great, God is good . . ." At bedtime, "I prayed the Lord my soul to keep."

I might as well have been recanting the ABCs or reading the phone book. I felt no connection to God, no communion with the sacredness of life.

Instead of repeating a bunch of worn-out, has-been lines that somebody else made up, I should have jumped upon my bed and bounced my thanks to the Creator. I could have bounced "thank you" for the thirty-two fireflies I caught that night. Bounced "praise" for the purple Schwinn Billy Blotsky let me borrow. Bounced "sorry" for the naughty word I called my sister.

But no, it was the same old "Now I lay me."

Jean Houston once said that we're boring God. Here he created this mind-boggling world with 25,000 species of orchids, lands as diverse as the Gobi Desert and Mount Fuji, and all we can do is mindlessly recite, "God is good, God is great."

When done properly, prayer is an act of spiritual intimacy, a profound expression of gratitude and respect. It's like a calling card. It hooks us up with the big guy. It opens us to Spirit's presence, lets us commune with something big and wide and brilliant.

In ancient cultures, art was always the mediator between man and God.

Before priests convinced us we had to have a go-between, we interacted with God ourselves by prayerfully dancing, chanting, and making masks.

Today, dervishes still spin their prayers. African tribes drum theirs. Tibetan monks make mandalas and Navajos paint sand. All are sacred acts, a powerful method for communing with the maker.

Kafka called writing his prayer. Jazz saxophone player John Coltrane prayed with his music.

"My goal is to live the truly religious life and express it through my music. My music is the spiritual expression of what I am, my faith, my knowledge and my being," Coltrane said before he died of cancer at age forty-one.

It's no wonder his music is still being played today. At St. John's African Orthodox Church in San Francisco, his music is played for an hour at each Sunday service. Parishioners even pass out music lessons along with counseling and hot meals.

Duke Ellington is another jazz great who turned to religion in the later part of his career, blending belief with music as he created "Sacred Concerts," which were large-scale efforts to explore the idea of God through jazz.

Russian composer Sofia Gubaidulina once told *The New York Times* that she writes music to serve God. "I can't think of any way to explain the existence of art other than as a means to express something greater than ourselves. I can't reach a single musical decision except with the goal of making a connection to God."

Art—whether it's cave paintings or toe-tapping gospel music—is our pathway to God. When done with the reverence and respect

225

it deserves, it liberates us from the alienation we all feel. It provides magical moments of transcendence, prophetic insight into new ways of being.

Try all you want, but years of religious study and "Now I lay me"s will never take you to the peak like a good piece of art.

Adriana Diaz ends her book *Freeing the Creative Spirit* with this vision for what she hopes will be the New Renaissance.

"Nuclear proliferation will turn into creative proliferation, destruction will be replaced by construction. Our descendants will read about how we began to carry pencils and sketchbooks everywhere. They'll learn how we healed ourselves and our cities by painting murals together and sculpting monuments out of recycled materials. As a world community we learned, for the first time, that the transformative power of the Creator is in the people. What a time to have been alive. They will say, 'It must have been great.'"

PAINT A PIECE OF CLOTHING

Paint Your Bootie

It doesn't matter what you paint—a hat, a pair of socks, an old
T-shirt. I once bought a bolt of 50 yards of heavy, white fabric. I
conned my mom into making dresses out of it and then I went to
work with the fabric paint. I love painting favorite slogans on my
clothes—things like "Create or Die" or "Any time not spent on
love is wasted."

More Fun Stuff

Have a board meeting with Benjamin Franklin, Thomas Edison, and other dead people you admire.

Come up with twenty uses for a pencil.

Dye your hair a color you've never worn.

You're in Good Company

Five Oscars were awarded to James Brooks's *Terms of Endearment*. You might think he'd have enjoyed the process. But every day, he said, was sheer mur-der. "It was like walking into a pro-peller. I was always aware of how bad it might have been."

And yes I said yes I will Yes.

HALLELUJAH

Hey you!

Yeah, you with the tiny dab of peanut butter on the end of your necktie. And you, miss, the one who wouldn't take your Cinderella costume off for eight whole days when you were in second grade.

Do you not know who you are?

Do you not know that you are God's beloved son, the greatest masterpiece that the finest creator ever made? Do you not know that your only calling, the only reason you walk this blessed globe is to magnify the Lord?

What are you so worried about? Why do you settle for crumbs? Content yourself with mundane musings?

This world is an immense treasure box, filled with blinding beauty, with mouth-watering, knee-bending, tongue-twisting delights.

Your body is a divine energy field pulsing with unremitting madness, unspoken joy. And what do you do? Worry whether or not you've shaved your legs.

You are meant to rule kingdoms. To ride stallions. To dance with the lions and sing for the stars.

The dewdrops that glitter on the morning's clover are diamonds for your pleasure. The honey that bees spin in hives is a holy banquet for your nourishment.

Do you not know you have dominion over the entire earth? This feisty, groaning globe is your castle. The twenty-four hours of this day are your toys. Your only calling, the only thing you need do is celebrate, magnify your place in the divine ocean.

Say hallelujah!

But no, you insist on scraping mud off your shoes, penciling "to do" lists, sweating over how many deductions you can legally take.

Are you blind, man? Is there rust in your eyes? God has bestowed upon you His most magnificent gift. Why do you refuse to play? Refuse to say "Thank you!"?

An artist's job is to shout "Hallelujah!" Hallelujah to the highest host, hallelujah for the miracles that happen every day, at every second, underneath his worn-out Birkenstocks.

What are you looking for? Where is your gaze? Throw away your periscope with its tiny vision, its limited viewfinder. Gaze instead through the mighty spectacles of God.

Throw off the shackles of the past. Say no to the petty trinkets, the measly hoops you've been jumping through.

You are a prince. A princess. A king. This green and growing earth is your playground, a never-ending slippery slide that rushes into ecstasy.

Say yes. Say it again. Say it 40 times 40 until you mean it. Until the very marrow of your bones knows it like a holy chant.

The famous cellist Pablo Casals once said:

Each second we live in a new and unique moment of the universe, a moment that never was before and will never be again. And what do we teach our children in school? We teach them that two and two makes four, and that Paris is the capital of France. When will we also teach them what they are?

We should say to each of them: You are a marvel. You are unique. In all the world there is no other child exactly like you. In the millions of years that have passed there has never been a child like you. You may become a Shakespeare, a Michelangelo, a Beethoven. You have the capacity for anything.

That's why being an artist is such a sacred calling. We're here to wake the sleeping giants who have forgotten to say "Hallelujah!"

Shake us from our sleep, O mighty artist. Jolt us, poke us in the ribs if that's what it takes.

Uncork the champagne. Roll out the gold-glittered streamers. We've come to grow the holy vision of God.

Say hallelujah!

231

CREATE A COSTUME

Trick or Treat

Think Patch Adams! Or Halloween—which, by the way, happens to be my favorite holiday.

As I mentioned, Patch owns a gorilla costume. And his ex-wife once made him a Santa Claus suit that he wore for years.

Look what having a costume did for the San Diego chicken.

More Fun Stuff

Dress up like Elvis. Go dancing.

Stage a watermelon seed–spitting competition.

Come up with your own Native American name.

You're in Good Company

Mary Gaitskill, author of *Bad Behavior* and *Two Girls, Fat and Thin*, decided in her late twenties that nothing was working and that writing "was a waste of time. I told myself if I wasn't successful by thirty, I'd kill myself."

WEeK 42

You need a certain amount of nerve, an almost physical nerve, the kind you need to walk a log across a river.

MARGARET ATWOOD

COURAGE

Being creative is an act of great daring.

Every time we write or sing or paint, we put ourselves in jeopardy. We step out on the highwire and there's a whole circus tent of people watching.

It's no wonder we often chicken out.

Hunters call it buck fever—that unexplained paralysis that sets in when they're face to face with the big one.

Doing your art *is* the big one. It covers damned near everything—your need to be visible, your need to tell the truth, your need to make a difference.

Is it any wonder you're just a slight bit anxious?

Often, our fear shows up in disguise—as procrastination ("I'll work on scene three tomorrow"), being too busy ("I'll start the novel when the kids get in school"), depression ("I'll start painting when I'm not so blue").

234

Call it what you will, it's all the same issue.

Being creative is genuinely spooky.

First off, we risk alienation. As much as people idolize movie stars and best-selling authors who appear on *Good Morning America*, they don't really applaud the people in their own lives who hole themselves up to write poems or practice the guitar. When we create, we're often alone, transported to another world, a world that doesn't always include those within elbow distance. People sometimes feel threatened.

They'll say "right on" and "you go, girl" when you get something published or land a part in a play, but until that time, they tend to cast aspersive looks your way, raising their eyebrows as if you belonged to a tribe of African Pygmies.

When you create, you make yourself vulnerable, throw prudence to the wind, hold nothing back. Phil Collins compared it to going onstage with your trousers down.

As long as you keep your mouth shut, nod your head at the right time, follow the prescribed dos and don'ts, nobody's going to laugh, disagree, or scrutinize.

But once you write, say, or paint something, the masks come off. People are going to know. And that takes courage with a capital *C*.

It also takes courage to joust with your own terrors, confront your own truths. When you surrender to your art, you may just find that your truth contrasts with the persona you present to the world. As Faulkner said, "A book is the writer's secret life, his evil twin."

You might find out that, God forbid, you don't really want to do what society thinks you should. Emily Dickinson, for example, discovered through her poetry that she didn't really want to marry and keep house like her mother.

And it especially takes courage to stand up to those buggery little voices that keep telling you you're boring, the ones that insist you have no talent and that if you write or paint, you're risking

235

financial failure. It takes courage to rail against them, to forge ahead when they keep sticking their leg out, trying to trip you.

It takes courage to keep going when your work doesn't meet up to your expectations, when instead of getting Jane Austen, you get Barney's singalong. You've got to keep plodding ahead anyway.

There's a lot of rejection; a lot of times people are going to say, "Sorry, don't want it."

We must be courageous enough to forge ahead anyway.

We can't wait for our fear to subside. It won't.

Lawrence Block once said that fear and courage are like lightning and thunder. They start at the same time and although fear may get there first, if you stick around long enough the courage will eventually show up.

The Frame Game

Buy an old frame from a garage sale or a thrift store and paint it.

More Fun Stuff

Tie-dye your underwear.

Make your own wrapping paper.

Read five children's books.

You're in Good Company

Michael Lehmann, writer/producer of *Heathers*, *Hudson Hawk*, and *The Truth About Cats and Dogs*, was convinced his career was over after his student film *Beaver Gets a Boner* was panned unmercifully at his college.

WEEK 43

Everything you are and do and say is filled with God: the trees, the asphalt, the people fighting over Aqua-Net at Wal-Mart. That sounds silly, but silliness is just as important as love, just as important as tragedy.

DONALD ROLLER WILSON

PET ROCKS, NUTS, AND DUCT TAPE

When I was twenty-three, a fortune teller from Jamaica took one look at my left palm and pronounced that my biggest problem would be deciding which of my many interests to pursue. At the time, I was designing clothes (things like too-tight yellow jumpsuits with jacks and rubber balls on the zippers' pull tabs), playing rugby, writing articles, and trying to break into the world of incentive travel hosting.

Today, I still dabble in many genres. I've written a children's book, a screenplay, several novels, and hundreds of magazine articles on everything from bungie jumping in New Zealand to carpet buying in Morocco. In other words, it's hard to pin me down.

If you're having trouble pinning down the artistic genre you most want to pursue, maybe it's because your genre hasn't been invented yet. Perhaps you should consider making up your own.

239

Whole careers have been made from such innovation. Los Angeles artist Kim Abeles, for example, uses smog to make art. She cuts out detailed stencils and lays them outside on Plexiglas, where, before long, microscopic bits of car exhaust and factory emissions collect. From smog, she has stenciled everything from tables complete with dinner for two in murky brown to a series of presidential plates. Woodrow Wilson, who encouraged responsible industry in his inaugural address, only stayed out in the smog for four days. George Bush, on the other hand, got forty days.

Chris Wink, cofounder of the Blue Man Group, a New York–based performing arts trio, said that although he was attracted to the arts, he didn't have the skills to be a fine artist.

"People talk about following your bliss, which is wonderful if your bliss happens to fit into a neat category like, 'I want to be an evolutionary biologist.' I couldn't follow my bliss, because I had blisses."

As a performance artist, he paints himself blue, drums, comments on contemporary culture, and catches marshmallows in his mouth.

"At a certain point, I made my brain a secondary organ and listened to my gut: 'Find a way to combine all your blisses and who the fuck cares if you're a waiter.' I had to rid myself of my immaturity and insecurities. I had to develop my own self," he says.

Writer Ted L. Nancy created a whole new genre of writing by sending ridiculously loony letters to various companies. With the support of Jerry Seinfeld, who first sent the letters to his agent, Nancy's letters were collected in a book, *Letters from a Nut*, that proved to be a phenomenal success. Here's one he wrote to a casino:

Dear Ms. Tilton:

I am a 675-pound look-alike for George Harrison.
I am in a group called the "Fat Beatles." We have
a tubby Paul who is 490 pounds. He is the cute
Fat Beatle. Do you want to see our tape?

> Sincerely,
> Ted L. Nancy

Nancy has written to the Coca-Cola company inquiring whether his beverage, Kiet Doke, interferes at all with their beverage; to the San Diego Padres asking if he can come to a game with a portable shower on his head (his medical condition requires that his head be kept in a vinyl enclosure), and to the Hyundai corporation wondering where he can buy their folding car that fits in pockets.

Or consider Tim Nyberg and Jim Berg, the duct-tape guys who sold 300,000 copies of their literary masterpiece, *The Duct Tape Book*, with a hundred and some uses for duct tape.

They even inspired a wannabe, the recently published *Ductigami*, a book with 101 ways to fold duct tape. In case this opus hasn't made your bookshelf yet, let me just tell you that duct tape can be folded into everything from a work apron and a beer bottle holder to a wallet and a baseball cap.

Seinfeld asks in his introduction to the second *Nuts* book, "Instead of being sidetracked with these imbecilic missives, shouldn't people be doing their jobs and contributing to the growth of our nation?"

In other words, isn't all this silliness a waste of time?

I think not. In fact, I'd venture to say we need *more* silliness, more willingness to look like a crackpot.

The word *silly* was originally a Middle English word, *sillig*, that meant "blessing."

241

If all of us would be willing to do three silly things a day, things like attaching toilet paper rolls to our feet or howling on traffic-jammed freeways (things humor consultant C. W. Metcalf did to overcome his case of terminal seriousness), we would unquestionably receive more blessings.

We would be freer to break new paths, find new adventures. As creators, we are not here to do what has already been done.

Maybe all of us should loosen up a bit and hitch our dreams to a sillier star.

As a song on one of my daughter's tapes says, "Boom, boom, ain't it great to be crazy?"

WRITE A SHORT STORY

nce Upon a Time . . .

It won't be graded. You don't even have

to show it to anyone if you don't want

to. But write something—maybe a story

about a favorite piece of clothing or your

last job interview. Natalie Goldberg sug-

gests taking the first half of your sen-

tence from a newspaper article and fin-

ishing it with an ingredient listed in a

cookbook. Play around.

More Fun Stuff

Give to charity all the clothes you haven't worn in a year.

Do the hokey-pokey in the produce aisle at the grocery store.

Stand up right now and proclaim, "I am a masterpiece. There is no one like me."

You're in Good Company

Georgia O'Keeffe was a commercial artist for years before she gained the strength to paint what she really wanted.

BELIEVING YOU CAN

If you grow up in small-town Kansas like I did, you don't meet many filmmakers. Or actors. In fact, the only "artists" I ever saw (forget meeting) were the Ink Spots, a group of semi-professional has-beens who came to Ellsworth, Kansas (pop. 2,500), to sing their one hit, "If I Didn't Care," and dedicate the new gymnasium.

Because the average person doesn't interact with artists, we don't think of art as something possible for us. It never occurs to us to try to paint or make a film or write a play. We think of ourselves as "normal" people—people who teach school or drive buses or wait tables.

Artists are different—mysterious, dark, brooding geniuses—definitely not somebody like you or your Uncle Seymour.

The media does nothing to dispel this air of mystery. They show us glamorous digs where famous writers and actresses take their vacations and tell us stories about their oddball iguana collection or their two hundred and eighteenth body piercing.

We forget that they're human beings who probably eat Post Toasties and oatmeal for breakfast just like we do.

We forget that making a film or writing a book is a process, a process that any of us could master if we wanted to.

The only difference between Woody Allen and you and me is that he believes he can make a film.

You and I believe we can *see* a film. It never occurs to us to make one. We wouldn't know how.

But get this: You didn't know how to ride a bike either—until you learned.

Making anything—from a chocolate mousse to a birdhouse to a five-part miniseries—has a recipe. Anyone who follows the recipe, learns the process, can produce the art.

Betty Edwards, author of *Drawing on the Right Side of the Brain*, compared it to reading. We wouldn't dream of giving kids a stack of books and expecting them to read. We wouldn't say about those who didn't pick it up on their own, "Well, poor thing, must not have the aptitude for reading." Yet that's what we do with drawing or painting.

We all learned to read. We can all learn to produce art. It's a simple matter of learning the process and mustering the confidence to give it a whirl.

Don't look at the projects in this book and think, "Oh, I could never write a country-and-western song" or "I don't know the first thing about dancing." Remember what God said to Howard Finster, the Baptist preacher turned painter, when Finster told him he didn't know how to paint:

"How do you know?"

How do any of us know unless we try?

Woody Allen recalls the exact moment he first believed he could make a film. He was eight years old, watching Tyrone Powers in *The Black Swan*, a swashbuckling pirate movie. He remembers thinking to himself, "Hey, I could do this." It was not a revelation that sent him out to find a movie camera, but it planted a seed—a seed that called to him, a seed that said, "You are capable of telling a story in this way."

Another time, when walking home from a movie, he found a strip of a half dozen frames of 35-millimeter film near the theater's trash cans. It had broken off the feature, *Four Jills in a Jeep*, with Phil Silvers and Carmen Miranda. He was mesmerized by the sight of the characters as he held the celluloid strip up to the sun.

In seeing that snippet of celluloid, he came to realize that movies aren't just magical fantasies to see on a Saturday afternoon (of course, he was also famous for seeing them on Tuesday, Wednesday, and Thursday afternoons, when he was supposed to be in school). They're created by human beings and there's a process for making one.

A process that he, Allen Stewart Konigsberg, small-potatoes boy from Brooklyn, could probably master. So what if his Jewish family was struggling, so what if he hated high school, dropped out of Brooklyn College? He, Allen Konigsberg (he didn't take his stage name until 1952), believed he could do it.

It's a startling revelation to most of us—that we could be filmmakers or painters. But it's the place all of us must start.

As long as we see art as something above us and artists as different than us, we will never be able to create our art.

Luckily, Woody Allen lived in New York City, where brushing elbows with real artists was likely to happen. Once, when he was fifteen, he was at Manhattan's Circle Magic Shop trying to decide what to spend his few dollars on (he was an avid amateur magician in those days), and in walked Milton Berle, the most famous comedian of that time. He joked with Berle and realized that Berle wasn't all that different from one of his uncles.

247

Here's to taking the frosting off the art world. Yeah, artists are prophets and visionaries and great talents, but so are you.

Or to put it another way, here's Jane Lazarre, author of *The Mother Knot* and other books:

> The assumption that art was a regal robe which fell upon your shoulders magically, bestowed upon you as an heir apparent rather than achieved through slinging the pickax across your shoulder every morning and making off to the mine, was revealed as the greatest hindrance of all to artistic work.

START A DREAM JOURNAL

Sweet Dreams

From this rich, interior life, you'll get all sorts of images and ideas for drawings and paintings and stories. Put the journal and pen by your bed and tell yourself as you're dropping off to sleep that you're going to remember your dreams.

Learn to say "I love you" in five languages.

Memorize three clean jokes.

Feed a stranger's expired parking meter.

You're in Good Company

At the end of his career, Jackson Pollock couldn't work at all. He'd stare at his empty canvas and tell friends that he "hated his easel, hated art."

Week 45

SAYING YES

Madeleine L'Engle once said that every piece of art, whether it is a work of great genius or something very small, came to the artist and whispered, "Here I am. Give birth to me."

The artist then has the choice, of course, to either respond with "My soul doth magnify the Lord" and willingly take on that work or she can say something like "Sorry, Charlie. Next time."

Usually we don't say it in so many words. In fact, we don't respond at all because we're not really sure we heard the idea. Who am I, after all? Or we hear it, but we're not sure it would really work. We wonder if we have the skills to do it.

We tell the idea, "I'm breaking up with my boyfriend right now. Kinda preoccupied" or "I'm busy with committee meetings and I'm up for a promotion at work and . . . well, it's a great idea and I'll do it later."

Unfortunately, ideas can't wait. They find somebody else. Somebody who has the time and the willingness to serve as channel.

Now.

Somebody who will write the next *Sesame Street*, the next *Prophet*.

Now.

My friend Kitty and I came up with the idea of selling pet insurance twenty years ago. Did we market it? No. Were we upset when somebody else did?

Not really, but we still talk about it.

If only we'd jumped on that idea when it came to us. If only we'd gone ahead and made some calls, written a plan. We'd be millionaires. If only . . .

There are literally thousands of ideas circulating in the universe. They come to us like light-footed butterflies flitting from flower to flower. If the flower says yes, the idea will stay, take root. If not, no biggie. There are thousands of other flowers to try.

Butterflies don't play favorites. It's the idea, not the bearer of the idea that's important.

"But I don't know enough to write the next *Ally McBeal*!" you still insist on wailing.

Butterflies don't land on flowers that don't have the pollen they need. The great spirit didn't give you that idea without the means to see it through to completion.

That's where your faith comes in. You don't have to take on the whole project right now. Just mix the paint, fill the ink pen, pluck the strings. Don't judge. Don't stop. Just do it and get out of the way.

Sure you feel inadequate. That's practically a spiritual prerequisite. That way you can depend on the idea itself (it knows more than you) or the muses or, better yet, the God that waits inside of you.

That's what growing is all about. If you say yes to the idea, it will stretch you. It will require new ways of being, new ways of seeing. It will take time. It will take dedication. But isn't that what you're looking for?

It's ironic. We read self-help books. We moan about our weaknesses. Yet, when given the chance to make changes, to become the "bigger self" of our destiny, we dig in our heels like a two-year-old.

Think of an acorn. Inside its tiny shell is the making of an entire oak tree. It can sit around for years, hidden in a squirrel's nest or a little boy's pocket. But once the conditions are right, once it's planted in the soil, given sunshine and water, it will grow into a towering tree. Guaranteed.

It just needs the right conditions.

That growing life force is inside of you, waiting for the right conditions. Yeah, you can wait. Stuff it inside a squirrel's nest. Jam it into a pocket. But eventually, it will find the right conditions. It will bloom.

Next time an idea whispers in your ear, take the time to listen. Invite it home for dinner. Say, "Yes, I'm willing to try."

PAINT A CHAIR

A Chair-Raising Experience

For years, I've bought old wooden chairs (average price? five
dollars) and repainted them in vibrant, southwestern themes. I
thought I was pretty clever until a Kansas City charity hosted a
fund-raiser by first luring
local artists to paint
chairs and then
auctioning them
off. The variety
was astounding.

More Fun Stuff

Write a fan letter to yourself.

Come up with five new outrageous
affirmations.

Pretend to be your favorite actress or
actor today.

You're in Good Company

Says Bonnie Raitt, "I think too much and judge
too much. It's terrifying when coming up with something new."

255

WEEK
forty-six

And yet they, who passed away long ago, still exist in us, as predisposition, as burden upon fate, as murmuring blood, and as gesture that rises up from the depths of time.

RAINER MARIA RILKE

A PROUD TRIBE

Becoming an artist is a little like joining the Lions Club. The secret password is "I want to be more." The secret handshake is "I believe."

The only dues are the ones you pay to yourself, the time you set aside to "be alone" and "to listen." The initiation is the agreement to see something bigger, to delve deeper when convention says, "That's all there is." While others try to close the book, the artist opens it, says, "There are more pages possible."

To say yes to the muse that whispers ever so quietly in your ear is a sacred covenant. To say "Here I am" to any art form is to join a powerful brotherhood.

It's to come face to face with Greco, Rumi, Shakespeare, to put on the cloak of Gauguin, Gilda Radner, Peter Gabriel. It's to join a proud circle with many members of all places and times.

Go to these brothers of yours, these kindred spirits, and study their ways, learn from their successes and failures and then add your quota. They have left stones for you to step on, footsteps to follow. Do not worry that you have nothing new or original to add.

All of us, when we first decide to write or paint, are inspired by someone else's writing or painting.

Filmmaker Myles Berkowitz, who recently released the quirky documentary *Twenty Dates*, was studying political science at the University of Pennsylvania when he happened to catch a midnight screening of *The Graduate*.

He was so moved by the film that he suddenly knew what he wanted to do with the rest of his life. He describes it as "being bitten by a vampire at night."

Eric Clapton says he was inspired by John Lee Hooker, B. B. King, and Buddy Guy. Of course, now, he's gone on to inspire legends of musicians who are making music today.

"I often feel I've been handed something to carry on in this generation. I feel a strong sense of responsibility. It's like carrying a torch," Eric Clapton says.

At first, we might copy the torch of our heroes, try to emulate their style. There's nothing wrong with this. Imitation is natural and necessary to the beginning artist. Even young Picasso painted in the style of his contemporaries for the first few years of his budding career.

Eventually, however, when we stand long enough in the commitment, our own style and voice will step forward to take its rightful place in the totem pole of progress.

In the inspiring movie *Amistad*, Cinque calls on the wisdom of his ancestors. He knows that their strength resides in his very bones. All he has to do is call it forth.

Likewise, in the Disney movie *Mulan*, the title character calls forth her ancestors to help her fight her battle with the Huns. Granted, it was a wisecracking dragon given voice by Eddie Murphy, but it was an ancestor with the soft eyes of historical perspective nonetheless.

257

In this book, I'm going to encourage you to stand on the shoulders of the artists who have gone before you. Hold fast to your spiritual heritage. Being an artist is a noble profession, a sacred calling, and all the wisdom of the brothers and sisters who have gone before you is in your bones.

Take their hands and let them help you across the chasm.

WRITE A
LETTER TO THE
EDITOR

Of All The . . .

There's something that really bugs you, something that's been eating at you for months. Instead of silently stewing, now's the time to give your two cents' worth. Who knows? The editor might even print it.

Find a tree to decorate (à la Christmas) in the park.

Pull something out of the trash and make something with it.

Wear something that doesn't really "fit" the dress code.

You're in Good Company

Stevie Nicks gets so nervous before going onstage that she shakes too hard to put on her makeup. For fifteen minutes, she's sick to her stomach. Stevie Nicks always said she considered herself a good songwriter, but not a very good musician.

Here, when the danger to his will
is greatest, art approaches as a
saving sorcerer, expert at healing.
FRIEDRICH NIETZSCHE

ARTIST, HEAL THYSELF

Therapists spend years digging up issues that
will surface immediately when you first attempt
to paint or write. They're all there—unworthiness,
the fear of not measuring up, the compulsion to
eat a bag or two of barbecue potato chips.

Here you are painting a stupid still life of ba-
nanas and mangoes, and every single block that
has ever prevented you from leading an exciting,
fulfilling life shows up to hang its laundry.

It's kinda like *This Is Your Life*, the TV show
where old friends and teachers show up to surprise and embarrass you.

"Hey, remember me?" the voices of shame
and guilt call from backstage.

As singer/songwriter Iris DeMent says, "You
got your good days and your bad days right there
in a little three-minute song."

And you paid how much for a shrink to de-
termine that your major problem is you don't
think you're good enough? Naming the problem,

admitting that you eat or run or whatever it is you do when you're scared is always the first step toward healing.

Notice I said the *first* step. It's always important to name a problem. I am an alcoholic. I suffer from depression. I was abused by my stepfather.

That doesn't mean you have to pitch a tent. We get so mired in the study of our diseases, in our human frailties that we forget the part about our divine magnificence.

Here we are reading books about how powerful we are, doing positive affirmations, pasting little stickies to our bathroom mirrors, but we're still getting up every morning and repeating something like this:

"I am the adult child of alcoholic parents, the product of a dysfunctional family, terribly codependent. I have to be careful of the small self that will lead me astray, the saboteur within that will separate me from my good, and the ego which will separate me from my God."

And the litany ends with something like, "But I am powerful."

What can your subconscious mind do but say, "Bullshit"?

The mighty river of God flows through your soul, the infinite power of the universe pulses in your heart, and you want to be "a survivor"?

You are not your stuff. You are not your history. You have the power to heal, the power to make radical changes.

Carl Jung once said that we will never heal our problems on the level they were created.

When you write a poem or sketch the new puppy born to the neighbor's Australian shepherd, you come to realize that you're more than the depression or the rheumatoid arthritis.

The act of creating taps the healing God current that runs through all of us. This is the level that has the answers. It's the level that can't be reached through our peabrain minds or our ego. It certainly can't be reached by looking at yourself in the mirror and affirming, "I am a survivor."

The act of creating drains away pay-the-rent, do-the-laundry details. It taps the deep subterranean impulse that recognizes magic and beckons us to wholeness. It repairs the defects.

Instead of telling everyone about your problems with your boyfriend, how he won't commit or how he falls asleep every night watching Jay Leno, why not write a poem about it instead? The poem may just take you to the other side.

My friend Bob had just been dumped by the woman of his dreams. He was feeling crazy—you know, that "I'll show her" kind of crazy. He knew he didn't really want to go there, so he wrote a poem that at first poured out all his pain, but then moved to this feeling of lightness, this crazy-elephant, squish, eel-piss place that made him laugh and realize how much more he really was.

Performance artist Chris Wink put it like this: "Follow your muses instead of trying to solve the social wounds of your adolescence. We've lost a whole generation of people who are dealing with their environment by retreating, by going into therapy. So instead, you go to open mike at a crummy tavern and perform your art. Rather than being introspective and constantly working on your shortcomings, get angry, get excited, get social."

There is so much more inside you than you ever imagine. You fear you are shallow and little only because you won't or don't look.

Creating something will give you a voice.

HOST A SHOW-AND-TELL

Stick Together When You Cross the Street . . .

Remember that essay *All I Really Need to Know I Learned in Kindergarten*? Well, the reason that story was so popular is because it struck a chord. What else really do we need to know?

This week, invite your friends over, ask them to bring something they value, and take turns talking about it. You'll be amazed at how much fun this is.

More Fun Stuff

Buy tomato plants for all your friends and take them over with three recipes.

Learn all the native flowers of your state. Find at least five of them.

Make a paper airplane out of brightly colored paper.

You're in Good Company

"All my life, I've been frightened at the moment I sit down to write," says Gabriel Garciá Márquez.

WEEK 48

Like a loyal animal,
the imagination will come when it
knows the door is open.

CAROL LLOYD

POWER OF THE PURPLE CRAYON

My favorite how-to book will never be found in the self-help section of your local bookstore. It was written long before the term *self-help* was even coined.

It's a children's book called *Harold and the Purple Crayon*, and it says more about the possibilities of the human condition than anything positive-thinking Norman Vincent Peale could ever cook up.

Written by Crockett Johnson in 1955, this little sixty-five-page masterpiece tells the story of a little boy named Harold who decides to go out for a walk one evening. When there isn't any moonlight (and, of course, everyone knows a good walk requires moonlight), Harold just takes out his purple crayon and draws the moon.

He also needs a sidewalk (which he draws) that leads to a forest (he only draws one tree because he doesn't want to get lost) that turns out to be an apple tree (or at least it is after Harold's crayon gets hold of it). Unfortunately, the apples aren't ripe yet, so Harold draws a frightening dragon to guard the tree.

When he falls into the ocean, Harold is able to grab his wits and his purple crayon to draw a boat and set sail for a beach, where he draws a picnic lunch with nine kinds of pie.

The whole book is about Harold's great adventures scaling a mountain, soaring in a hot-air balloon, and touring a city, all created by his ever-faithful purple crayon.

It's a powerful book because it demonstrates a great spiritual truth—we are the authors of our own lives. We draw every detail—even the dragons and the oceans we "accidentally" fall into.

Harold could have gone on his walk, noticed there was no moon, and sat down and pouted. Isn't that what most of us do? Damn, no moon. I'd better call my therapist, hit some pillows. He could have drawn his moon, compared it to El Greco, and said, "I am a hopeless sham. I'll never be an artist."

Instead, he kept reaching for his purple crayon and drawing every event, every answer, every friend that he needed. We all have that power—not only with our art, but with our thoughts and with our yearnings.

Harold and his crayon also remind us of the butt-kicking power of our imaginations. We can strike out for the Great Wall of China, lunch at the Savoy, fly a glider down the Pacific coast, strangle lions at the Strand, and still be back at our desk for the ten o'clock meeting.

Joanna Field says this about the imagination:

> The ordinary everyday perception of things which serves us pretty well when going about daily practical affairs is not the only kind of perceiving the mind can do. . . . Only a tiny act of will is necessary in order to pass from one to the other, yet this act is sufficient to change the face of the

world, to make boredom and weariness blossom into immeasurable contentment.

Just because something doesn't exist on the material plane does not mean it's without value. Perhaps it has even more value.

When Joan of Arc was being interrogated by the church, she said, "Of course God speaks through my imagination. How else would God speak to me?"

Harold was only a kid. He hadn't yet lost his imagination, his sense of wonder and awe. No one had explained yet that he couldn't have whatever he wanted. As long as he had his purple crayon, he could ride the universe.

In today's world, crayons and creativity might as well be the same thing. How many adults do you know that still have crayons?

Remember that big box of Crayola crayons with sixty-four colors—everything from apricot to fuchsia to forest green? With that one small gold and green box you could have anything your little heart desired—navy blue carousels with peach prancing ponies, magenta castles with yellow-green drawbridges, puffy white clouds and purple grass although your teacher might have frowned on that kind of thing. Grass is green, don't you know.

Each year of school, however, the Crayola stash gets smaller. By the time we graduate from high school, we're wielding nothing but a blue Bic for figuring our checking account.

Let's go out this week and get some crayons. Let's create our world the way we want it. And if we happen to fall into an ocean or run into a dragon, we'll just draw ourselves a lifeboat and head for the beach, where at least one kind of pie will be waiting.

MAKE A COLLAGE

Potpourri

Grab a bunch of old magazines and start ripping. If you're really stuck, make a collage of all the things you want in your life— your "wish list."

Take a card table to the park and host
a gin rummy tournament.

Pull something out of your pantry
and draw it.

Eat something you've never tried.

You're in Good Company

Steve Winwood was kicked out of the Birmingham
and Midland Institute of Music.

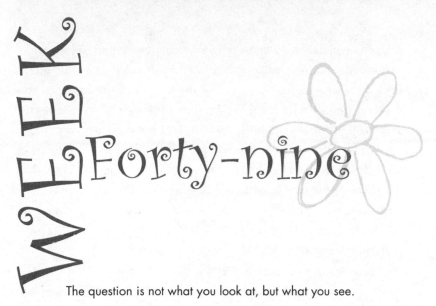

WEEK Forty-nine

The question is not what you look at, but what you see.

HENRY DAVID THOREAU

REVERENCE

Anne Lamott says in her wonderful book *Bird by Bird* that a writer's job is learning to be reverent.

"There is ecstasy in paying attention," she writes. "You can get into a kind of Wordsworthian openness to the world, a sign that God is implicit in all of creation."

She says this awe is easy to see in a child (or when you're with a child who says "gee whiz" at everything from the burned-down house to the dirty dog), but it's also available in a chipmunk, a dark cloud, and the woman who puts on her crazy red hat and walks to town.

The trick is to open your eyes and look.

Most days our rational mind is so busy jawboning about the boss who doesn't appreciate us or the car that needs tires that we forget to really see.

Betty Edwards wrote a book back in the '70s called *Drawing on the Right Side of the Brain*. It ended up being a huge best-seller, not because everybody in this country wants to become a cartoonist or draw portraits, but because learning to draw offers the gift of true sight. Many of the book's fans were lawyers and doctors, people who used the lessons of drawing to open themselves up to the astonishing details of their everyday lives.

I'm always shocked at the number of details I've been missing when I sit down and actually commit things to paper. The other day, I was drawing Tasman as she painted on the easel I gave her for Christmas. Drawing a five-year-old, by the way, is almost as challenging as trying to draw Mexican jumping beans. That's probably why painting students start with still lifes.

As I began to draw the jeans she was wearing, I noticed the pointed pockets in the back, the double stitching down the seams, the rock she had picked up at the park and stuffed into her pocket. Before drawing, they were just a pair of brown jeans with an infuriating zipper that never stayed up. I found myself falling in love with those jeans and feeling even more love for that darling five-year-old who wore them.

In Edwards' book, she shows many examples of "before" and "after" drawings done by students when they started her program and when they finished, six weeks later. The difference was startling. It was like looking at something Alfred E. Neuman might draw and then Picasso. Every one of her students, she claims, makes similar strides.

And the reason? They simply took the time to see. Edwards claims anyone can draw once they learn to see. It's no different than learning to write your name.

Because there is so much input in the world, our brains look for ways to lump things together. It's easier for the conscious, rational part of our brain to place things in easily identified categories. For example, the conscious mind sees a bag lady on the street. It's easier to shove her into a category—"she's homeless" or "she's street scum"—instead of really looking at her as a unique individual with a mother somewhere that used to sing her lulla-

272

bies, as a former waitress who lost her husband to bone cancer when her twins were first born. Putting her in the "homeless street scum" category makes it easy to process, easy to get on with it.

I'm not shaking my fist at the rational brain. That's its job. The rational brain has lots of input coming at it and it has to group things together quickly. It's like when you're moving—you throw all the shoes into one pile, all the underwear into another. It makes it easier to box them and get them where they're going.

But if you really want to write or draw or make a movie, you must take the underwear and the shoes out of the box and really look at them.

It all comes down to seeing. Once you see—I mean *really* see—reverence is a piece of cake.

DO A PERFORMANCE PIECE

Street-Corner Magician

Okay, so just what is a performance piece? For one thing, you could dress like Elvis and go dancing. You could paint yourself blue and do mime in the park. I saw a human jukebox once in San Francisco. Well, actually it was a refrigerator box decorated like a jukebox. The guy inside sang requests depending on which slot you put your dollar through.

More Fun Stuff

Learn to say "hi" in sign language.

Go to a restaurant in a part of town you've never been to.

Write a poem about your favorite relative.

You're in Good Company

Laurence Olivier said, "Stage fright is always waiting outside the door, any door, waiting to get you. You either battle or walk away. It can come at any time, in any form."

WEEK 50

Rejoice that rain and wind, sun and sky, earth and sea still thrum
with profound, undiminished urgency in your bones.

BOB SAVINO, *AS THE SPIRIT MOVES*

BELIEVING IN MAGIC

Jack Smith, head writer for *The Young and the Restless* and creator of *The Bold and the Beautiful*, credits his Catholic upbringing for the mystery and magic that enable him to write five hundred episodes of soap operas a year.

"You've got to believe in the magic, in the mystery of making something from nothing," he says. "For me, it all started growing up in the Catholic church. There was such a mystical bent to it.

"When I was a kid, I really believed that when that priest blessed the bread, it became the body of Christ. When he anointed the wine, it was the blood of Christ. I was so drawn in, I was completely captivated by this religion of magic.

"That ability to see magic is what it takes to be a writer, to find mystery in the most mundane," Smith says. "You have to find a joy, to be able to dig deep, to see a cathedral inside a tree."

Although Smith has expanded on his early Catholic beliefs,

he has never lost his ability to see magic, to see cathedrals inside trees, inside the characters that he writes about every day.

To Smith, they're like a group of friends that he really cares about.

"You have to continually go deeper, but you never get bored as long as you do."

The trick is being in the present moment. In fact, that's the first thing he teaches writers he trains for the soap opera that has ranked number one for ten years.

"When I look at the literature I love, the movies that really speak to me, it's always so obvious that the writer was right there in that moment and nowhere else," he says.

Not that it's always easy to stay in the moment. Smith admits to being a very future-oriented person, but he tries to remember to "breathe in, breathe out" and "be" right where he is now. He has studied with Thich Naht Hahn, a Buddhist monk who teaches this mindfulness.

Smith says he also prays every morning when he heads to his studio at 5 A.M.

"I pray for spiritual enlightenment. I pray for some magic to happen. I don't know how or why or even who I'm praying to or even what this enlightenment is, but I have a strong feeling of that 'power' being in me and in all my characters," he says.

He says he doesn't always start out feeling it, but if he sticks with it, it invariably surfaces.

Showing up is the key. Smith is in his studio writing by 5 A.M. every morning, five days a week.

"Discipline is everything," Smith says. "You can't sit around and wait to get motivated. You act first and then the motivation comes. If I sat around waiting to be motivated, I would never get anything done."

He also touts the discipline of chewing off small pieces.

"I could never write five hundred soaps a year if I thought about it. I doubt I could even write one episode," he says. "I always break it into pieces. If I were to sit down and tell myself that I have to write thirty pages of dialogue and direction today with four acts and it has to be done by the end of the day, it would be a struggle.

"Instead, I'll say something like 'I'm going to write this prologue and that is it.' If I drop over dead afterwards, I will have accomplished everything I want to. I'm going to put everything into this prologue and that's all I have to do," he says. "It's a mental game, but it makes it a pleasure and a joy for me."

Of course, after that, he does the same thing with scene one, scene two, and so on.

And from that tiny step-by-step M.O., Smith has created a very successful career. Not only has he was won three Emmy Awards, but he has complete artistic control over what he writes. *The Young and the Restless* has been the number-one soap opera for ten years. *The Bold and the Beautiful* comes in a close second. Smith has the money to pursue other projects, such as American Hawaiian Leis, which ships leis from his adopted home of Hawaii to the mainland.

Tiny baby steps. One foot in front of the other. Stay here. Right here. And write your prologue.

COME UP WITH A SHOW IDEA
FOR JERRY SPRINGER

No Way

Create a character who could appear on Jerry Springer's show and send a letter from him or her requesting an audition. If you do get on, you've just landed your first acting gig.

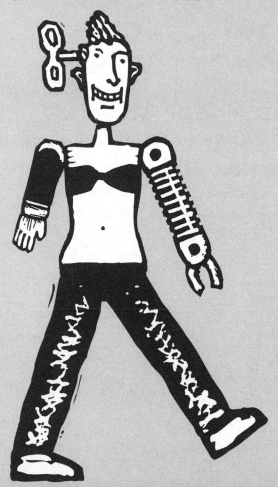

TUNE IN NEXT TIME FOR:
My Secret Life as a Cross-Dressing Robot

Wear your pajamas to the movie theater.

Learn a card trick.

Sign up for Spanish (or French or German) lessons.

You're in Good Company

Norman Mailer didn't even submit work to Brooklyn High's literary magazine. He says he wasn't even remotely the best writer in his class. A teacher at Harvard called his writing only "fair."

Week 51

SEEING WITH THE HEART

Yeah, yeah. You've got 20/20 vision. It says so right on your driver's license.

But do you really participate in what you see? Or do you see what society prescribes that you "see"?

William Blake, the English poet, called our so-called 20/20 vision "the guinea sun" mentality.

"When the sun rises, do you not see a round disk of fire somewhat like a guinea [a British gold coin]?"

Oh, no, he writes, "I see an innumerable company of the Heavenly Host crying Holy, Holy, Holy, is the Lord God Almighty."

We tend to think of our vision like a camera, registering the unalterable "facts" of what is out there. We see the giant E at the top of the eye doctor's chart. Period.

But more is out there if you make the choice to look for it. As a creator, you have the ability to take anything and lift it to an exalted state.

In fact, that's the artist's main responsibility. To see the divinity in the discarded chewing gum wrapper, in the hot fudge dripping down the side of your eight-year-old's face, in the pile of papers stacked on your desk.

The Australian Aborigines have a ritual called Dreamtime, where they go into a deep, trancelike state. Not only do they by-pass the normal ways of seeing things, but they draw specific information that's not available to the body's five senses. A tracker, for example, can follow a trail that was left months ago.

Michelangelo claimed to be guided by something he called *intelleto*—an intelligence not of the rational mind, but a vision-ary intelligence. He saw things beneath the appearance. An artist, therefore, uncovers something as yet unborn, unseen. We have the ability to "see" things not readily available to the five senses.

This creative imagination opens us to insight and a deeper, bigger consciousness.

As it is now, we see only what we've been taught to see. Ob-jectivity, son, that's the American way.

We've learned to block out things like angels and magic and divine beauty. That's a guinea sun. Can't you see what it says on the chart?

According to the police of social and political control it's a bunch of nonsense to see your own personal imprint or, even worse, to see God in the sun.

But it's the real truth, the higher truth. As artists, we must open to this larger, higher truth. We must look with our hearts and see the bigger picture. Michelangelo's *intelleto* is available to all of us. We can tap into this insight, this God picture. More accu-rately, we must learn to be tapped, to receive.

It is only through passion and desire. But if we have the de-sire, we can, to quote Blake once again, "melt the apparent sur-faces away and display the infinite which is in all."

MAKE A GREETING CARD

When You Care Enough to Send the Very Best . . .

A card can do everything from propose a tryst to celebrate an anniversary to console a pal who lost a pet. Make a card for somebody who needs a boost.

More Fun Stuff

Create a library of inspiring books.

Write down every good thing anyone ever said about you.

Make a list of a hundred things you want to do before you die.

Pretend to be your favorite historical character.

You're in Good Company

"Writing is like making wallpaper by hand for the Sistine Chapel," says Kurt Vonnegut.

GET A LIFE

You dress like Ally McBeal, diet like Oprah, and know more about Bart Simpson than your own brother. In other words, you haven't had an original thought since Roseanne took to the airwaves in 1988.

This book, if nothing else, is about having original thoughts, about celebrating the unique and wonderful person that you've probably forgotten that you are.

Not someone you that you've manufactured to please your parents. Or your spouse. Or your boss. Or your tennis partner. This you, this unique, glorious, magnificent self, is the one that was planted in your heart on the day you were born.

You are absolutely unique, a one-of-a-kind miracle. Of all the billions of humans that have walked this planet, not one is exactly like you. Which gives you a pretty big responsibility, an important assignment. There's a special puzzle piece that only you can contribute.

Week Fifty-two

Unfortunately, most of us have lost our puzzle pieces, we've allowed our uniqueness to be smothered by a long list of self-negating assumptions:

"Oh, I could never do that."

"People would think I'm stupid."

"I'd make a complete and total ass of myself."

In other words, we've muzzled nearly everything that's creative and wild and fun. We've civilized the "naughty kid" who wants to run with a stick, self-inspect his diaper.

Only problem is it's the naughty little kid who likes to run into the street and fry ants under a magnifying glass that comes up with new ideas.

Think back to when you were a kid. The whole world was your palette. With one flip of the imagination, Popsicle sticks turned into magical airplanes that did flips and flew upside down. A bar of soap was the Little Engine That Could ("I think I can! I think I can!") or a limousine for a famous FBI spy. And the beach—oh, the beach—offered infinite building material. Remember the sand castle you built with moats, kings, ladies-in-waiting, and even a wizard? Back then, your imagination had no limits.

But then your parents piped in:

"Act your age."

"Don't talk with your mouth full."

"If everyone else stuck their head in a toilet, would you?"

And then teachers threw in their two cents:

"Paint between the lines."

"Make an ashtray like everybody else."

"Trees are green—not purple."

And then, just before you could do something really dangerous, your professors taught you about "real" art and literature, about metaphors and style. You finally realized how trivial your creative efforts were. After all, who are we compared to the great masters?

286

At work, of course, it only got worse. Unless you were the boss—the big, big cheese—your main job was to follow the rules. Hold the imagination. Besides, with overtime hours, kids to feed, and a mortgage, you probably didn't have time to play with bars of soap and sand castles anyway.

Before long, you realized you didn't even know how anymore. Alas, life's colors had dimmed, its mysteries had run dry. Your capacity to wonder, to be surprised, to be puzzled was long gone, buried in a box with your childhood Tinkertoys. Where's the remote control?

Some like to call this adulthood. Being responsible.

But I think it's more like a lobotomy—self-imposed surgery on everything that's natural and fun. The only thing that remains is the censor, the judge, the parent who reels us in before we get carried away.

I don't know about you, but I want to be carried away. I want to build sand castles, dance on tables, play hopscotch in my pajamas.

So what if society says these are useless pursuits, childish whims, a total waste of time?

So what if creativity doesn't guarantee security? I've had security and, believe me, it ain't everything it's cracked up to be.

Yeah, creativity is unknown, even dangerous. But I'm tired of putting my chair in a row, marching in a straight line.

I'm ready to zig, to say "yes," to make up my own dance.

Consider this your invitation to join me.

That naughty child that likes to dance loop-de-loop in the airport is never lost completely. He might be hiding, cowering in the basement. But he's there. Desperate for some attention. Eager to be invited back out to play.

MAKE
A MASK

Who's There?

Masks have been
around for at least
15,000 years, showing
up in cave paintings as
far back as Paleolithic
France. Yours isn't
going to be that old.
Make it with anything
that speaks to you.
Papier-mâché is
always good. There
are lots of recipes for
papier-mâché, but
I like this one:

> Flour
> (it's cheap)
>
> And water
> (it's even cheaper)

More Fun Stuff

Host a full-moon ceremony.

Create the perfect boyfriend for
TV's Ally McBeal.

Make a collage of something you want.

You're in Good Company

When an editor at Random House suggested changes
to Lawrence Block's first mainstream novel in the
1960s, he immediately went back to writing hack
fiction, the only thing he felt worthy of for many
years.

289

Truth is rarely safe or predictable. But by its danger, you will learn your love. **BOB SAVINO**

DIVING INTO THE UNFAMILIAR

Being an artist is not unlike being an archeologist. Day after day, you dig, sifting through the dirt, not exactly sure what lies beneath the surface.

At first, something compels you to start digging, maybe a shard of a pot. But then you find a bone and then a purple neon tooth. The original small piece of pottery might end up leading you to a dinosaur.

E. L. Doctorow, author of *Ragtime*, once said, "I've discovered that you cannot start a book with an intention, a calculation. You have to start writing before you know what you want to write or what it is you're doing."

Eventually, the dinosaur will reveal itself.

The important thing is to follow that urge that says "Dig!" In this day and age, that's not always easy. We want answers before we start. We want assurance that we'll strike gold.

But it's impossible to know. You might find lead or silver. You just don't know. But you've got to dig anyway. You've got to be like Mel Fisher, who every day for seventeen years went down looking for the *Atocha*, a gold-laden Spanish galleon that sank off the shore of Key West in 1622. Every morning, he'd get up and say to his crew,

"Today is the day." He was convinced he'd eventually find silver and gold (which he did), but he never knew for sure.

Oftentimes, we fool ourselves into thinking we know what we want to write or sing, we think we've got it all figured out. But as we start painting or drawing, something completely different shows up.

Anne Lamott compares it to waiting for a Polaroid to develop. "You can't—and, in fact, you're not supposed to—know exactly what the picture is going to look like until it has finished developing."

Sarah Ban Breathnach, who wrote the huge best-seller *Simple Abundance*, thought she was writing a book about simplifying your life.

She says in the Foreword: "The book you're reading now bears no resemblance to the book I began or to the book my editor expected. While I wrote for two years, *Simple Abundance* underwent an extraordinary metamorphosis, as did I. I began writing about eliminating clutter and ended up on a safari of the self and Spirit. No one is more astonished by this than I. *Simple Abundance* evolved from creating a manageable lifestyle into living in a state of grace."

If Breathnach has stuck with her original plans instead of surrendering to the Spirit that wanted its voice, the book would probably have already gone into remainders. She was willing to follow the voice that said, "Dig here, write this." She was completely willing to throw her original plans over the side of the ship like ballast she no longer needed.

If something is urging you to write or sing or dance or play your guitar, listen. Follow that voice. Maybe you're being asked to deliver the next *Prophet* or maybe you've got a poem that will someday heal a child from a broken home.

At this point, you don't know. You can't know. But the spirit that's compelling you to write or sing or draw has a plan, a pretty big plan.

It's like Doctorow said: "Writing a novel is like driving a car at night. You can see only as far as your headlights, but you can make the whole trip that way."

Write a love letter to your soulmate—
whether you've met him or her or not.

Wear your hair sticking straight up.

Write a book report.

You're in Good Company

Eudora Welty said looking at galley proofs of her
books gave her a terrible sense of exposure, as if
she'd gotten sunburned.

The beginning.